"In these times the notion of stories about priests interacting with children bring unwelcome images to mind, but we desperately need stories like Fr. Kleba's. His stories show us that enriching truly loving relationships within our extended church family are possible. It's no wonder the St. Louis affiliate of Voice of the Faithful® presented Fr. Kleba with its "Person of Integrity" award in 2011."
— Nick Ingalam, Public Relations Director,
Voice of the Faithful® National Office, Newton, Massachusetts

"This is an eloquent, heartfelt, vivid, funny, insightful, and deeply personal set of stories about the relationship of the author with children, ... It will, almost inevitably, be sometimes read against the background of the clerical sex-abuse scandals ... But it has nothing to do with them other than as an absolute contrast to them. The book is dedicated to all parish priests who faithfully dedicate themselves to imitating Jesus who took children in his arms and blessed them. ..."
— John W. Padburg, S.J., The Institute of Jesuit Sources, St. Louis, MO

"As we slowly recover from the past three decades revealing the failures of Priests' conduct with minors, this work is a blessing of monumental importance in restoring in the minds of the public an insight into the ministry of healthy priests in the care of minors. ... These stories repair in a graphic way the reputation of the priesthood in its call to minister across a broad spectrum of human need."
— Bertin Miller, OFM, Founder of RECON, The Wounded Brothers Project.

Gerald with his parents, Philip and Alice Kleba, at his first Mass at
Resurrection of Our Lord Church in St. Louis, Missouri, March 11, 1967.
PHOTO: ©1967 Robert Westrich, used with permission.

"Are You Still A Priest?"

TRUE *Stories of* **TENSION** *and* **TRUST**

GERALD J. KLEBA

Gerald J. Kleba

"Are You Still A Priest?"
True Stories of Tension and Trust
Gerald J. Kleba
GJK Publishing

Published by GJK Publishing, St. Louis, MO

Cover and Interior design:
Kathleen W. Herring, www.kathleenherringdesign.com

ISBN: 9781514399231

Publication Year 2015

Printed in the United States of America

www.GerryKleba.com

Dedication

To all parish priests
who faithfully dedicate themselves to
imitating Jesus who took children in his arms
and blessed them.

❖

"No experience was too insignificant—
the smallest happening unfolds like destiny.
Destiny itself is like a wonderful wide tapestry
in which every thread
is guided by an unspeakably tender hand,
placed beside another thread,
and held and carried by a hundred others."

Rainer Maria Rilke, *Letters to a Young Poet*

❖

Table of Contents

Acknowledgements

My sincere thanks to all those people who believed me when I said, "I am writing a book." On one hand, they respected my need for solitude. They were also filled with delight and excitement when I told them the topic was about relationships between priests and children. Highlighting those who encouraged me:

Editors: John Knoll, Ann Stephenson, Daniel Sheerin, Joan Barthel, and Anne Barthel. All of these wonderful people were more than editors; they were cheerleaders and promoters of the first order. Finally, kudos to my professional editor and proofreader, Lisbeth Tanz, who impressed me with her persnickety thoroughness. Cover photo: Robert Westrich. Design: Kathleen W. Herring with a little help from Cathy Davis — I am profoundly grateful to all of these dear people.

Technology assistants who were invaluable: John and Diane Gozdzialski and Dominic Soda. Without their help this book would not have reached the publication level this soon, and my patience would have been totally taxed much earlier.

Front row boosters who believed in me when I had hardly written a sentence: My sister, Mary Margaret Kleba, and other family members, Cori Rose Benitez and Jeanne Jensen and Jane Wingle.

St. Cronan Parish members who believed that the stories would promote healing in the church: Delores Blount, Pat Carter, and Saralou Hendricks were all very patient with me when I fell short of doing expected parish work.

I am grateful to all those people who told me that I was a good storyteller and reminded me that Jesus taught in parables.

Finally, there would be no book without the cooperation and support of all those individuals and families who are spotlighted in these chapters and agreed to have their family life exposed to the world. I am even more touched by the families of the children who have gone to glory: Jeremiah Busiek, Justin Jacob, Gari LaHay, Michael Potter, and Mev Puleo. Each of them had to relive some of their most tragic days and found it difficult to respond to my requests because they were not open to renewed pain in their lives. However, they each came to see this book as a fitting tribute and memorial to their child who might otherwise be forgotten. Without their help "Are Your Still a Priest?" could not have been written with all the authenticity, poignancy, and soul searching that is its hallmark.

ON HOLY THURSDAY POPE FRANCIS SAID

March 28, 2013—Holy Thursday

VATICAN CITY (CNS) — Pope Francis called on the world's priests to bring the healing power of God's grace to everyone in need, to stay close to the marginalized, and to be "shepherds living with the smell of the sheep. This is what I am asking you," he said with emphasis, looking up from his prepared text, **"be shepherds with the smell of sheep,"** so that people can sense the priest is not just concerned with his own congregation, but is also a fisher of men.

Surrounded by more than 1,600 priests, bishops and cardinals, Pope Francis led them in a renewal of their priestly promises. He focused his homily on the meaning of being "the anointed ones" through ordination, underlining Holy Thursday as the day Jesus shared his priesthood with the apostles.

The pope urged priests to not grow weary of people's requests and needs no matter how 'inconvenient ... purely material or downright banal," such appeals may seem. "Priests need to look deeper at what's driving the encounter" the person's underlying hope and desire for divine comfort, for being "anointed with fragrant oil, since they know we have it."

"We need to 'go out,' then, in order to experience our own anointing, its power and its redemptive efficacy to the 'outskirts' where there is suffering, bloodshed, blindness that longs for sight, and prisoners in thrall to many evil masters," the pope said.

Catholic Telegraph – http://www.thecatholictelegraph.com

Foreword

FR. GERRY KLEBA'S BOOK, "Are You Still a Priest?," is one that needs to have been written and his are stories that need to be told. The book follows Fr. Kleba from parish to parish and ministry to ministry over his 48 years as a Catholic priest and focuses particularly on his relationships of deep friendship with young people. A book about priests and kids? Oh, oh. Is this going to be another sordid account of clerical predators abusing altar boys and taking advantage of children in orphanages and outreach programs? Will we get another detailed account of hierarchical irresponsibility, with bishops and diocesan officials moving known predators from parish to parish, exposing yet another group of children and youths to men who have proven themselves an obvious danger to the innocent?

This book by Fr. Gerry Kleba is poles apart from such modern horror stories – shamefully true though they be – but a tale that is much closer to the lived reality of the vast majority of priests, children, and former children – that is, today's adults, in the Catholic Church. Fr. Kleba tells the stories of his personal and pastoral friendships with children, always including comments and corrections, where needed, by the "kids" themselves. The parish experiences he recounts include his time in small towns, inner city neighborhoods, and suburban parishes, a university stint, and hospital chaplaincy. The social justice issues in which he has involved himself include race relations, food pantries, nuclear waste, and clean water advocacy. He has taken part in working for women's rights and dignity in the Church and society; he has engaged in LGBT advocacy and been active in promoting ecumenical cooperation and interfaith understanding.

In this book he tries to show that in the context of the integrated and multifaceted life and ministry of today's Catholic priest, a bond of true friendship between priests and young people is not only possible, but is in fact a specially blessed relationship brought about by God's

Spirit, meant for the spiritual enrichment of both parties, and for all those who their lives eventually touch.

I write both as someone who has been a priest for 48 years and a child for the usual period before that. So my earliest experience of the priest-child relationship was as a child. I grew up in an active Catholic parish (actually two, our original parish was split and we wound up in the new one) in St. Louis, Missouri, in the 1940s and 50s. We were lucky – we had really good priests in both parishes. They led us in our worship of God and taught us catechism in our parochial school (an event that fell somewhere between an impromptu holiday and a celestial visitation), but that was only the beginning of their presence in our lives.

Whenever there was a baptism, graduation, marriage, anniversary, or death in the family or neighborhood, the priests were around to bless the occasion with their words of faith. When someone was taken to the hospital because of injury, heart attack, or simply old age, the first phone call was always to inform the rectory of the details, in full confidence that one of the priests would soon be by with communion and consolation. When family arguments turned violent or someone got drunk and was committing mayhem, the first phone call was again to the parish house; the police were only brought in after the priest carried out his role as first respondent, peacemaker, and Solomonic judge. Parish picnics, carnivals, bake sales, Holy Name Society, Knights of Columbus, teenage dances, softball and soccer games, Sunday afternoon movies, altar society sessions, Perpetual Help devotions, Vincent de Paul and Legion of Mary meetings would have all been incomplete without the presence of the parish priest. He was at least expected to "stop by," although it was understood by all that he might not be able to stay long. If the priest was late arriving on the scene, you would always hear the murmur, "Where's Father?" in tones of annoyance or concern.

It all fit into a comprehensive view of faith. For us kids, the parish priest was our own representative of Jesus Christ in the neighborhood. He was Christ and he was ours. He showed us what Christ was like:

available, accessible, understanding, gentle, intelligent, humorous, generous and, most of all, reliable. You could count on him when you needed him. He was the one person we felt we could trust completely, with our sins, doubts, moments of confusion, our crises at home and school, and our hopes and plans for the future.

Like most Catholic boys my age (no girls allowed in those days), my first introduction to the priests was through serving Mass. Memorizing the incomprehensible mumbo-jumbo of the Latin responses was an introduction to a mysterious world of things one believed but didn't try to understand. Learning to watch for two fingers touching the altar cloth as the sign to ring the bell was an initiation into a sacred responsibility that permitted no childish distraction or daydreaming. Learning to move the heavy missal from one side of the altar to the other – climbing, descending, genuflecting in the middle without tripping over one's cassock, then climbing and descending again – was an exercise in esoteric gymnastics that stamped one's Catholic boyhood as "complete."

Serving Mass taught us that worshiping God was serious business. Arriving late, slovenly dressed, poorly prepared, or fooling around were invariably noticed and reprimanded. On the other hand, being an altar boy was considered a privilege and offered such perks as excursions, swimming parties, special breakfasts and, most of all, a chance to be friends with the priests. For beyond all the other things the priests did for us, they were, above all, role models. How many millions of Catholic men in the United States had their first "grown up" conversations about life, God, morality, as well as sports, politics, and movies, with their parish priest? It was no wonder that many young boys in my time wanted to be priests. We saw it as a good way of life, serving as Jesus' local representative, someone who fulfilled an indispensable function in our neighborhood.

After 8th grade, four boys from my parish entered the minor seminary to study for the priesthood, but I was not one of them. I had my heart set on going to the Jesuit high school as my older brother had done, so I did not sign up in time for the minor seminary. Then my conscience began to bother me and I began to think, "What if I had a vocation and didn't follow up on it?" Fortunately, the parish priest was there for me and had common sense. He assured me that I would get a good education at the Jesuit high school, and I still had plenty of time to decide whether I had a vocation to be a priest. Four years later, after high school, I entered the seminary.

I offer my childhood experience of relating to our parish priests because it is so typical of Catholic children of our day. I am aware that the picture, as it appeared to my youthful gaze and as it remains in my memory, was somewhat idealized. I have later learned that the priest, at the beck and call day and night from needy parishioners, was a prime candidate for burnout. With no family of his own, he often suffered from loneliness and emotional deprivation. Some took to drink. Others became judgmental martinets, petty dictators and micromanagers. Still others threw themselves into building schemes, adding structure after structure to the parish complex, only to watch bitterly as the parish was consolidated or shut down years later when the neighborhood changed. Some found happiness with a good woman; they left the active priesthood and married, while never giving up the hope that they might someday be able once again to serve God's people in a priestly ministry.

And some, stunted in their sexual instincts and cynical in their use of power, preyed upon children and vulnerable adults. These men were statistically very few, but far too numerous in terms of the harm they did and the scandal they caused. They not only violated young lives and caused psychological harm from which many of their victims never fully recover, they also violated a sacred trust from which the Church does not know how to recover. We have moved from a naively confident atmosphere of "If you can't trust your parish priest, who can you trust?" to the hermeneutic of suspicion taught in abuse management seminars: "You must avoid not only intimacy with children but even any appearance of intimacy."

In this light, Fr. Kleba's book is the reminder we all need that the relationship between child and priest is one that is typically initiated by God and blessed by God. The stories recounted in Are You Still a Priest?

will be immediately recognizable to Catholicism's former children and to its priests who look back on their years of priestly ministry. They are stories of common sense, basic instinct, and deep spiritual commitment that together provide the strongest guarantees that the friendships and counseling relationships between priest and child will not deteriorate into a predatory, exploitative interaction. Healthy priests and healthy children will find in these tales an affirmation that they can trust their instincts in these friendships, that God's grace is at work in every truly Christian relationship between children and priests.

"Are you still a priest?" "Why are you still a priest?" Such interrogations will continue to be put to priests today by modern people. Such deceptively simple inquiries often conceal the real nature of the doubts harbored by skeptics inside and outside the Church: "Is it possible to remain a well-integrated and joyful person while serving God's people effectively as a celibate priest in today's world?" "Is it possible for an adult priest to maintain deep personal relations with children and young people which are not manipulative or exploitative, but rather expressions of God's generous grace and occasions for spiritual and psychological growth?" In seeking an experiential response to these and similar questions, one can do no better than to peruse and enjoy Fr. Kleba's Are You Still a Priest?

Thomas Michel, S.J.

"Are You Still A Priest?"
True Stories of Tension and Trust

"People who set themselves up to judge us from some remote distance, sitting in a comfortable office where they do the same routine tasks every day, cannot begin to realize how 'untidy,' how scattered our daily work can be. We can barely manage our ordinary parochial round, the kind of thing which when it is strictly carried out—makes a superior exclaim: 'There's a nice well-kept parish.' There remains the unforeseen. And the unforeseen is never negligible. Am I where our Lord would have me be? Twenty times a day I ask this question."

The Diary of a Country Priest, Georges Bernanos, 1936

I AM NOT A COUNTRY PRIEST or a city priest. I am both in addition to being an academic and a hospital chaplain. I'm typical of the 38,275 ordinary, no-name priests in the United States who serve families and love children as Jesus did. According to Vatican sources there were 412,236 of us on planet earth in 2010. My stories are the stuff of priestly life across the country. With the tragedy of the abuse scandal, people are hungry for my hopeful stories of wit and wisdom and tension and trust that make Jesus alive in the twenty-first century.

Some skeptics inquire, "Why are you still a priest?" I am still a priest because I am happy being a priest. According to the Dalai Lama, "If you want to be happy practice compassion." I am compassionate, suffering with others; and I am even better at rejoicing and celebrating with others. After forty-eight years as a priest, I am more loyally in love with God and God's creation. I am a priest committed to the mystery of dying and rising, even when I was told that I faced incurable cancer. Failure, even death, is not an option for me but merely a transformative mirage, a speed bump on the road of life. I am a lemonade maker, squeezing life's lemons as they roll my way. I celebrate success salvaged from possible failures. Thomas Edison said, "I have not failed. I have just found 1,000 ways that won't work."

Finally, I have put on the mind of Christ, committing myself to the social change of the gospel. I stand up for justice in our world and, given the unity of all creation, I am one with Archbishop Desmond Tutu, Dr. Martin Luther King, Jr., Pope Francis, Mother Teresa, and Aung San Suu Kyi of Burma. I am in solidarity with equally dynamic people dedicated to ecology, the women's movement, the Lesbian, Gay, Bisexual, and Transgender community, and the interfaith and ecumenical sphere. I have been an actor doing my bit part to make these women and men shine on the world stage. Steve Jobs said, "The ones who are crazy enough to think that they will change the world are the ones who do."

Because of the news headlines, priests today are frequently scrutinized or ignored like a vestige from a bygone era. Bernanos talks wryly of the oversight given by diocesan superiors who sit in their offices some remote distance from the daily chores of priests and the tasks that go unnoticed. This is the 'untidy' scattered daily work: Mass, Sacraments, prayer, faith formation, buildings, grounds, insurance, security, meetings, visits to the sick and homebound, food pantry, Vincent de Paul Society, doorbells, lost and found, weddings and receptions, meetings, funerals with meals and social time, finances, bills, taxes, salaries, meetings, spiritual development, homilies, writing and editing parish publications, meetings, days off, vacations, exercise, doctor visits, emergencies, and still meetings on top of more meetings. Performing these well might get a priest the ecclesiastical accolade: "There's a nice well-kept parish."

I have seldom gotten that seal of approval. Some of my unpopular pastoral activities have challenged the church's social injustice. Instead of accolades, I have been chastised and threatened with suspension by a ranking prelate. I avoided that judgment with the help of a canon lawyer costing me $1,000.00 a month, half my monthly salary.

For seven years, a distressed parish was unable to pay my salary. When I sent in the annual financial report, the diocesan treasurer discovered an error in a column of expenses because of a numerical typo. He criticized both my math and my typing but he never noticed the zero in the box marked "pastor's salary." That box was on the top line. His eagle eyes overlooked the zero on all seven previous reports. During those seven lean years family and friends supported me.

Bernanos continues, "There remains the unforeseen. And the unforeseen is never negligible." An unforeseen negligible is insignificant, not worth considering, unimportant, inconsequential. But the unforeseen "something" is never negligible, never too tiny or too trivial to overlook. When a priest is to be attentive to these minor details, he is driven to the Bernanos prayer. "Am I where our Lord would have me be?" Twenty times a day I ask that question.

The unforeseen, never negligible, is the stuff of this book. It fits under one single heading—fear. Scripture says, "There is no fear in love; but perfect love casts out fear" (1 Jn 4:18). I am constantly discovering how little I know of perfect love. I struggle with fears regarding race, gender, age, income, education, wealth, health, looks, disabilities, status, locale, and still undiscovered bugaboos.

In our competitive milieu, these fears gnaw at me and cause stress as I compare myself to others. I address these fears in my stories. These never negligible issues emerge in all relationships but can become even more apparent with children. Children can be brutally honest, and I can be ever more guarded.

Again, twenty times daily I pray, "Am I where our Lord would have me be?" Many of these tension-filled stories focus on sick children, five of whom died. While I survived these situations, I did so a changed man. I could have become reclusive and guarded, but that was not my choice. Instead of recoiling from the loving commitment that involves suffering, my commitment to the mystery of dying and rising moved me to participate selflessly in the abundant Christ life. My longing for growth and maturity demanded that I double down on vulnerability.

These intimate situations could have led me to despair or to holiness, which is the moral drama of life. I have repeatedly found happiness, not through material gain or renown, but through a life reaching out to catch the other who is falling, even as I myself stumble. I am formed by suffering service. I am made better. I answer the question, "Am I where our Lord would have me to be?" Yes, I am still a priest.

JOHN NICHOLS

*"I will give you fifteen facts and one story. If the story is told well,
it's the story people will remember."*

Ronald Reagan

*"There is no agony like bearing the burden
of an untold story within you."*

Zora Neal Thurston

YMCA 1992

YMCA 1992 IS THE SIMPLE ENGRAVING on a wide burnished brass frame a
5 x 7 black and white picture of nine-year-old John Nichols, shoulder to
shoulder with me on a playground bench with a basketball balanced on our
knees. We were in the yard of St. Bridget's Church, where all the windows
are covered with a heavy wire mesh screen to keep balls and vandals from
breaking in. Since that photo was taken, there has been a dramatic shift in
the way the world views little boys sharing a park bench with a priest who's
dressed in a casual pullover and a Roman collar.

I was pastor of an inner city parish in an African-American
community in St. Louis. In the 1990s when I was pastor there, one of my
commitments was serving as a board member of the Downtown YMCA.
In that position, I had the good fortune of naming some of the children
who would receive scholarships to attend YMCA Camp Lakewood for
one week during the summer. John Nichols, the boy on the picture, was
selected.

When John's week at camp was over, he wrote a letter of thanks to
the YMCA for this all-expense-paid Outward-Bound-type experience. It

was a week without the pollution of the city, the sounds of gunshots and the sticky asphalt of a steamy St. Louis summer. In fact, many of the ghetto youngsters were more at home with the harshness of the inner city than they were with the insects, birds, and creepy-crawlies of the Ozark hills, lakes, and woods. It was a star-studded week, looking heavenward into the pitch night sky and into the eyes of the stellar counselors who both challenged and encouraged the campers. The glaring light pollution in the shadowy city was often used as cheap burglar insurance, but at Lakewood, bug repellent was the only insurance needed.

One day as I was finishing my Y swim, Larry Alvey, the president of the YMCA of Greater St. Louis stopped me and told me about a thank you letter from a boy at our school. He was very impressed and asked me if I could get permission from John's parents to use the letter and a picture of John in the YMCA annual report. John's parents agreed and hoped it would insure John's selection for another scholarship. A few weeks later, they sent a photographer to take the picture that would grace the cover of the 1992 YMCA annual report. Several months later, the president gave me a framed picture and asked me to give a copy to John along with the report so that he could see himself as a cover boy. I accepted the pictures immediately and then had a second thought and handed them back.

"I have a better idea than me merely handing this picture to John on Sunday after Mass. He'll take it, glance at it and might forget to show it to anyone when he got home. I think that we ought to pick a time when you could come to the rectory after school. We could have a party and John could invite his family and some friends and I will invite the church staff. We will have some ice cream and cookies and then you can make a presentation and even read John's letter so that some of the other fourth graders can realize how important it is to write a thank you card. We will make a real presentation like an Academy Award ceremony." He agreed to my idea. The parish staff helped me put the dining room in party mode. We got balloons and several flavors of ice cream.

The following week, John and his big sister, Kiesha, and several of his classmates came to the party with his grandma. Sister Gail, the school

3

principal, was there to add support and authenticate the educational and religious value of this prestigious affair. I introduced the Y president, Larry Alvey, who was standing at the head of the dining room table. He was formal and dignified in his suit and tie, cuff links and buffed shoes. He was a prominent white man standing to honor a small, brown skinned boy who was shy, soft-spoken, well-behaved and unobtrusive. President Alvey held up a copy of the published annual report and said that the best story in the magazine was inside the front cover. Then he read John's letter entitled *"A Thank You From A Happy Camper."* He proceeded to read the entire letter that John had written praising his counselor and the programs at Camp Lakewood. He continued, "I am here today to tell you that this is one of the coolest things that I get to do with my job. I get to see that the generous support that St. Louis citizens give to the Y permits youngsters like you, John, to go to camp on a scholarship and have such a wonderful experience out in the country with other children who are different from you. Now John, it is my pleasure to give you and Father Gerry a gift as a memento of this day." He handed John and me a wrapped present. I watched the gleam in John's eye as he opened his present. He tore off the brown wrapping paper and ran his finger over the shiny brass frame. It was the posed photo of us sitting on the bench with the basketball in my lap. YMCA – 1992 was engraved and oxidized on the bottom center of the brass frame.

We thanked the Y president for coming and the room cleared out just as soon as everyone made sure that the plates of cookies were mere crumbs. John was about to leave also, but I told his family to wait for us in the hallway. I sat next to John and looked him in the eye. We were alone in the dining room with the table cluttered with ice-cream dishes and crumpled napkins. I pushed them off to the side so that our precious picture was the center of attention. I asked him, "Do you know what that magazine is with our picture on the cover?"

He shook his head and sheepishly said, "No" as if he had missed the answer to a classroom question that he should have known.

"Let me tell you how important this magazine is. Each year, the YMCA publishes this report telling about all the swimming lessons, sports leagues, latch key programs, and summer campers that they provide to the whole St. Louis area. And they send this to all of the people who donate money to help kids like you. Some of the richest and most generous people in St. Louis are going to get a copy of this with our picture on the cover. So that means that thousands of people who don't know us at all only know one thing about us. What do you think that they know about us, when they look at this picture?"

John was even more sheepish this time with an answer, because he knew that he missed the answer to the last question. He answered me with a question. "They know that we're friends?" he guessed with a question mark in his treble voice.

"John, you've never been more right in your whole life." I stood the picture of us up on the white table cloth. I repeated, "The one thing that they know about us is that we are friends. As long as anybody has this picture, and however old we are, that is what they will know; we are friends. John Nichols and Father Gerry Kleba are friends," I emphasized. "And do you know what a friend always owes his friend?"

John was still cautious and even more hesitant. "That .. they will... stay friends."

"Right again, John." I squeezed his arm and shouted like a game show announcer. "John, people know you by the friends that you keep. Have you ever heard anyone say that?"

"Sister Gail says that at school and my grandmother says it too sometimes."

"John, since we are on this picture together, for as long as we live we are friends, and people will know us as friends. I want to tell you that I will never do anything to embarrass you as my friend, and I ask you to promise me that you will only do things that will make me proud of you. Should we shake hands and promise this to each other?" We both clutched hands with our elbows on the table in an arm wrestling pose to show our solidarity like brothers. You could almost hear me think the Boys Town slogan,

"He ain't heavy; he's my brother." We rose from the table and I walked John down the hall with my hand on his shoulder. When his grandma and Mary Jane had finished talking, I showed them to the door with a farewell ghetto handshake with the finger clasp and the fist bump.

Ten years after that YMCA - 1992 cover photo, in January 2002, *The Boston Globe* ran a huge front page exposé on Catholic priests that has made the terms "pedophile priest," "child abuser," and "cover-up" horrible and commonplace short hand for the Catholic church in the U.S. I noticed our YMCA photo on my piano room bookcase twenty years later in 2012, and I thought that this idea of highlighting a black boy with a white man, a Catholic priest as an influential YMCA board member and the intimacy of our close presence to each other was a great idea (with fund-raising capabilities) in 1992. In 2002, a mere one decade later, it would be viewed as verging on criminal behavior. Today, no development director for any youth oriented charity could keep a job by proposing such a picture even for the back cover of a brochure. People might look at our picture and accuse me of "grooming" a youngster for indecent treatment. As a priest over forty-eight years, nothing could be more tragic and heartbreaking to me. The timeline by decades was disastrous. In 1992 — The YMCA photo. In 2002 — *The Boston Globe* Sunday headline and cover story. In 2012 – High ranking church leaders convicted and imprisoned for enabling child abuse. I think that I speak for many priests and for countless people, Catholic or not, when I say that it is time to reframe the story and correct the generalizations that depict priests as threats. It is time to rise up out of the ashes.

During the writing of this book, I was committed to finding each child and youth so as to share their chapter with them. I also wanted to invite their corrections and receive their approval for publication. I was able to locate everyone — except John, the young boy I had been pictured with in 1992. Since it was the picture of John and me that initiated this endeavor, I was disheartened that I was unable to locate John. I asked people at St. Bridget's and received off-hand responses from people saying that someone had seen John on the

Metro downtown or someone was linked to John on Facebook. But no one could get John's phone number for me. I was becoming desperate because this key story was such a good introduction to my book. Without John and the YMCA — 1992 story, the effort would likely fall flat. When I was about to despair about finding John, I was invited to a Jazz Concert with many St. Bridget's members. At a break between sets, I shared my story of frustration. I told them about my writing project and my frustration searching for John. Oliver Grant, the man who had been the parish and school musician for many years told me, "My daughter will find him on Facebook in fifteen minutes." A police officer told me, "If he has a driver's license, I'll find him as soon as I get back to work." Both of these conversations were encouraging. I was plagued by one thought that lurked in my mind no matter how I tried to suppress it. A black boy growing up in the ghetto might be a grim statistic. He could easily be dead or in prison. I took heart in that each of my earlier unsuccessful inquiries provided some positive response concerning John's whereabouts, and no one mentioned anything negative like arrest or jail or death. I consoled myself with the hope that "no news is good news" and the people of St. Bridget's would have their finger on the community pulse and knew if sadness touched any of the families. While all those conflicting notions barraged my brain, I now had some hope.

The very next day Oliver called me with good news. He said, "My daughter, India, found John on Facebook."

Since I didn't even know the right spelling of his common last name, I still wasn't convinced. "Oliver, how do you know that you found the right John Nichols?"

"Father I called and said, 'John, this is Oliver Grant. Do you remember me?' And he replied, 'Mister Grant you used to play piano for the school Masses.' So he's the right John Nichols and he told me to give you his phone number. He has a job and children."

I was delighted. Just as I was about to lose hope, I got this incredible call. I had found the last person that I was searching for, the subject of my

7

first chapter. I hadn't seen John since I left St. Bridget's in 1995. I called John and we planned to meet at a local Penn Station restaurant.

He was late and my nagging fears started to return. I studied each person on the parking lot imagining what John might look like twenty years after our last encounter. Then I spotted him getting out of an old sedan. He was still tall and slender as he had been in his youth and once I saw him I remembered his narrow slit eyes and comfortable, but not bubbly smile. We embraced as if no time had gone by, and he apologized for his tardiness. I admitted my nervous worry and how I almost gave in to the temptation to leave. We went in and ordered our lunch. I was hesitant to ask anything about his mother because she had led a difficult life and most of John's upbringing had been in the hands of his grandparents. However, when I inquired about his sisters, he brought his mother into the conversation, so I knew that John was in contact with her. He told me that she still lived downtown and was a cancer survivor for six years. He worked the three to eleven shift in a suburban factory and he went to visit her every morning to see that she had eaten breakfast and then again in the evening after work to make sure that she was safely in bed. "If I go there and she is asleep, I don't even wake her. I just leave and go home knowing that everything is secure." I was amazed at the vigilant compassion he displayed for his mother when he had to care for his own two children, one three years old who was also named John and a new baby, a girl six weeks old, and their mother. John was keeping his nose above water financially and seemed surprisingly calm and well-balanced emotionally. In terms of gospel values, he scored off the charts, five stars, a perfect ten performance. John's favorite bible verse must have been James' letter saying, "True religion is this caring for widows and orphans in their distress and remaining untainted by the world."

John wasted little time in asking me, "Are you still a priest?" His forthrightness took me aback because I had never seriously considered anything other than the priesthood. I wondered why anyone would dare raise the question. I told him an abbreviated version of my priestly life since St. Bridget's and a shortened version of my health history and my lung cancer scare. I highlighted the fact that I was a published author and how I was confident that this book featuring his story would certainly make the bestseller list.

John also inquired about Sister Gail, the school principal. The last time he saw her was four years ago when he and a friend were driving by the school and decided to stop. He found Gail walking down the hall. "She was the first person we saw, and she said 'Hi' calling us each by name. Maybe she…" his voice trailed off. "Maybe she loved me more than anyone in the whole world."

We spoke some more about the picture and the YMCA. I had planned to bring the picture but forgot. I apologized for that, and John admitted that he didn't remember the picture or the conversation. But he did remember the week at camp and the party in the rectory dining room. What more was a fourth grader supposed to remember?

Before long, John had to go. We returned our trays to the counter, headed for the parking lot and talked about our shared excitement at finding each other. I gave him my card and invited him to come to Mass at St. Cronan's. "If you come here, I will introduce you as one of the stars of my book. I promise you a standing ovation."

He responded, "I might shock you by coming. I don't get to church since I work six days a week and have so many family things to do." I knew God understood, and I personally wanted to lead the cause for John's canonization while he was still alive. I was really in awe. He is quite the young man, strong and compassionate, surpassing all my hopes. I laughed at myself for all the fears, (arrest, jail, death) that I had when my search for him led nowhere. I also reminded myself of the futility of worry and always assuming the worst in every situation. We said our farewells with a hug rather than the friendship pact handshake of twenty years earlier. I knew my friend, John, was a good father and son. John knew that his friend, Gerry, was a good priest. Both of us kept our promise.

IMPORTANT NOTE

In the writing of this book I committed myself to finding each of the children and youth and sharing their chapter with them and inviting their corrections and approval for publication. I have made all the corrections as faithfully as possible. All of this has taken place with each of the stories included here. If the child has died his or her parents and/ or spouse has approved the chapter that features his or her life and our relationship.

Washington University Hospital
Pastoral Care

ST. LOUIS CHILDREN'S HOSPITAL is a part of the Washington University Medical Center, the largest Saint Louis hospital, which is annually adjudged to be one of the top hospitals in the United States. While it was founded in the late 19th century, it was only in the 1960s with Vatican Council II in the Catholic Church and new ecumenical awareness in the National Council of Churches that a better spirit of interfaith cooperation developed. This saw the appointment of a full-time Catholic Priest on the hospital pastoral team and as a deacon I was assigned to help him with this massive endeavor. It was in this new situation of tentative cooperation that I responded to the invitation to go to the side of the stressed Dennis family when infant Tommy was clinging to life by a mere thread.

"BE SHEPHERDS LIVING WITH THE SMELL OF THE SHEEP"

Pope Francis said, "When a priest "doesn't put his own skin and own heart on the line, he never hears a warm, heartfelt word of thanks from those he has helped. Stay close to the marginalized and be shepherds living with the smell of the sheep." Homily at Holy Thursday Chrism Mass in St. Peter's Basilica, March 28, 2013.

In the *Saint Louis Post-Dispatch* Sylvester Brown, Jr. wrote: **"Priest works to save bodies and souls by giving blood.** An odd thought struck me as I stood in the back of Immaculate Conception Church of Dardenne on Sunday morning. The moment of divine clarity came as the band and choir engaged in spiritual harmony, as sunlight poured through the church's circular, stained glass window, reverently emphasizing the massive wooden and ceramic cross on stage. Standing in front of the edifice, a priest dressed in a lavish burgundy, gold, and white robe celebrated Mass.

"This is my body, which will be given up for you," he chanted as the congregation echoed his words. It was at that moment – sun shining, music sounding above, the priest standing with arms spread wide like the wooden image on the cross – the thought occurred to me: Hawkeye Pierce delivers one heck of a sermon.

The Rev. Gerry Kleba, 63, reminds me of Alan Alda, the actor who played Hawkeye on the old M*A*S*H television series. The 6-foot-6-inch priest with smiling, aqua-blue eyes and grayish-white hair looks more like today's "West Wing" Alda than the actor from yesteryear's M*A*S*H. Yet, it's his mixture of altruism and mischievous humor that brought the Hawkeye character to mind.

Kleba was the "guest priest" at Immaculate Conception Sunday. He called a few weeks ago to tell me he planned to donate his 200th unit of blood during a blood drive that day. Kleba has given blood, four or five times a year, since he was an 18-year-old seminary student.

Kleba may not be able to stitch and suture like "Hawkeye," but he's dedicated to saving lives in his own way....Several churches hosted "Catching up with Father Kleba" events Sunday. Kleba reminded parishioners that they were "continuations" of Christ's Gospel. His "good news" lives in us all, Kleba told the congregation. Donating blood is good news for those in need.

The room erupted in hearty applause after Kleba rose from the mobile gurney after giving his 200th unit. Red Cross executive, David A. Chumley, presented Kleba with a commemorative pin for doing more than just "talking" about donating blood."

December 6, 2005. p. 13.

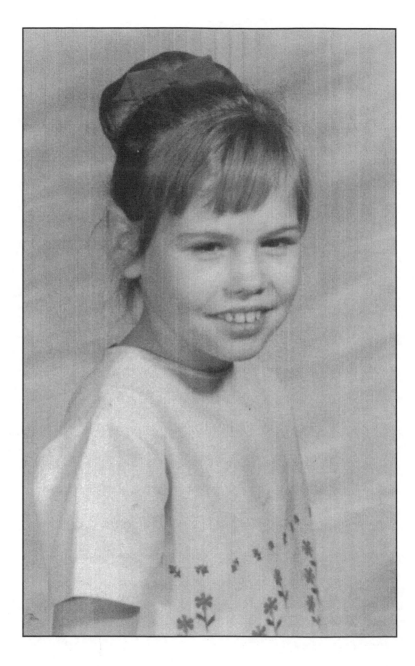

THERESA DENNIS

Dear Editor,

I am 8 years old. Some of my little friends say there is no Santa Claus. Poppa says, "If you see it in The Sun, *it's so." Please tell me the truth, Is there a Santa Claus?*

Virginia O'Hanlon

Yes, Virginia, there is a Santa Claus, *New York Sun, Editorial, September 27, 1897*

I WAS YOUNG, ENTHUSIASTIC, fervent, and fearless. I was a new deacon assigned to assist the Catholic chaplain serving at the largest hospital in the State of Missouri. Barnes Hospital, now Barnes/Jewish, and St. Louis Children's Hospital comprise the teaching hospital affiliated with the Washington University Medical School. It is annually awarded a high ranking by the AMA. I was not dry behind the ears and should have been scared sensible by the first patient that I visited. He was a muscular construction worker who had both of his arms burned off at the shoulders when the jack hammer he was operating encountered a high voltage wire under the street. The assignment did get easier, but that incident taught me to keep on my toes and get down on my knees.

I usually headed up to the patient rooms at about 9:00 a.m. after the doctors had made their rounds, the patients had their baths, and things were a bit settled. This particular Saturday, I got a call from Ginny Laughna, a nurse at Children's Hospital. She told me a family was there with a very sick baby, and they needed a chaplain. I asked if the family was Catholic; she said that they were not. I told her to call the Protestant chaplain, because back then there was a wide wall of religious separation before ecumenism broke the icy barrier among many Christian denominations. Besides that general atmosphere of hostility, there was a deep fault line between Catholics and Protestants in

15

this health care institution. Although it was a thousand bed hospital in an overwhelmingly Catholic city, it had only recently invited a Catholic priest to join its pastoral care team. Ginny explained to me that she had called the Protestant chaplain and that he had refused to come, "because these people are poor and he doesn't come for people without money." Adding insult to injury, he concluded, "they're not even from St. Louis, but farmers from southern Illinois."

I told her, "Call the chaplain once more, because I don't want to be accused of stealing sheep. If he doesn't come in fifteen minutes, call me back and I'll be right over." I only lived a block away. The Protestant chaplain still refused, so I headed to the intensive care unit at St. Louis Children's Hospital.

Ginny was a young blonde with a winning smile balanced with a professional approach to her serious task. She explained to me that I would be seeing a six month old baby named Tommy who was dying from a nearly always fatal lung disease. The profound sadness of this situation was compounded by the fact that Tommy had contracted the disease from his mother.

She had just cleaned the chicken house and returned to the house to find her infant crying and needing her attention. She washed her hands and went to him unaware that she was the carrier of a lung disease that one could contract around chicken dung. In the process of caring for Tommy, he inhaled this deadly virus that is now commonly known as hystoplasmosis. Infants were very susceptible to contracting the ailment. His little lungs were filled with the disease and his life was now rapidly drawing to a close. Ginny led me to a small bassinet covered with an oxygen tent and introduced me to the distraught, guilt-ridden parents. I embraced them in a group hug seeing the horror in their bloodshot eyes and sleepless faces. They were quick to tell me the story that I had heard moments earlier at the nurses' station. They explained their ignorance about such a lung disease. I tried to console them and relieve their anxiety, but they were not to be consoled or able to forgive themselves. Tommy

16

was at death's door, and it was up to me to pray him into the arms of a gracious God who was already smothering him with the fullness of love. Jesus had told his followers the importance of being like a little child in order to enter the Reign of God (Mt 18). Certainly, no one was more like a little child than a tiny infant like Tommy. In truth, I prayed more longingly for Tommy's parents and his siblings who would bear so much undeserved guilt over this sad situation. We stayed by the tiny bed as a doctor and Ginny monitored the situation keeping watch on Tommy's vital signs and comfort level. After a few short minutes, Tommy breathed his last. His tiny body, which had gallantly struggled to live, rested in the arms of his mother while his spirit was released to glory, surrounded by the angels in paradise. The dear parents wailed in anguish, and I held their quivering bodies close to mine. Tommy was at peace.

Some time later, Ginny reclaimed Tommy's lifeless body while I accompanied his parents back to the waiting room. It was quiet, and we were alone. They explained that they were taking Tommy home to bury him on their farm. The room was gray and unremarkable. Without windows, the only light came from buzzing, bright white florescent rods, which punctuated the worn look of the institutional seating. I said, "You've been inside for so many hours." I was careful not to say cooped up after I had heard about the poultry disease. "I suggest you go outside and get some fresh air. It's a sunny, blue sky day and right across the street is a lovely park. Go out there and walk or sit on a park bench for a while, because it will take the nurses some time to complete the paperwork before they can release Tommy to you. I'll walk you to the front door of the hospital. You can then cross the street with the stoplight."

I realized that a big hospital, a six lane street, and 1,400 acre Forest Park are all a little intimidating to a heartbroken rural farm family. But I knew that they would be no stranger to crisp, clear winter freshness. That would certainly be an improvement over the stuffiness of the waiting room. I ushered them to the curb and then awaited their return by the nurses' station.

While I was visiting with Ginny and the other nurses and catching my breath in this sad agony of infant death and self-blame, Ginny piped up and said, "When Tommy's parents get back, they are going to ask you a favor."

"And just what could that be?" I inquired. I was a bit taken aback by another request feeling I had done quite a bit already on an early Saturday morning.

"I'm not going to tell you, you just wait and see." Her response reminded me of adults playing the children's game, I've Got A Secret. I wasn't really up for games. When I was finished with this emergency I had done for a Protestant, I was committed to visiting Catholic patients in the adult hospital and bringing them Holy Communion. I was already an hour late in starting those rounds that usually took me until five or six in the evening to finish. It all depended on how much people wanted to talk and how tactful I was becoming in saying, "We'll have to stop now, because I have others to see. I will come back later and bring you Holy Communion." I was young, a people person and wanted to make everyone happy, so I wasn't very good at that particular separation spiel.

Tommy's parents returned, and I was prepared when his mom said, "Father, there is one more thing that I would like you to do for us."

I acted somewhat surprised and cordially responded, "And what is it that you would like me to do for you?"

"When we left home, our daughter Theresa gave us this letter to Santa Claus that she had written. We were supposed to mail it to the North Pole when we came to St. Louis. We would like to give it to you so you can play Santa and explain to her what happened to her little brother, Tommy." With that, they handed me that letter with more confidence than they would have had placing it in the mailbox.

I took the letter and assured them that I would do all I could to help Theresa understand. About that time, the hospital had Tommy's little body prepared for them to make the long ride to the farm. He had already made the longer trip to the other side in glory. They pulled the car up to the side door of the hospital away from the incoming traffic of visiting parents and family members. Ginny placed the tiny box on the mother's lap. She was sobbing as I kissed her drenched cheek, and the car disappeared into the Kingshighway traffic. I watched as the white puff of exhaust from their car disappeared, hopeful that the exhausted couple would stay awake for the long ride with their loved but lifeless passenger. Ginny and I walked back into the hospital very slowly almost fearing to return to the scene of such sadness. We hugged each other. We were both too young to see such senseless tragedy and youthful frailty. They were young parents left to deal with a tiny baby's final gasp. God, where are you hiding? I was ready to head to the adult hospital and make rounds, but I could feel the unmailed letter burning a hole in my pocket.

We returned to Ginny's station and stood side by side as I reached into my pocket to pull out the small white, wrinkled envelope addressed to Santa Claus, North Pole. It had a Christmas stamp on the envelope. I held the note close to my chest so that Ginny and the other nurses couldn't sneak a peak. "Now let's read this and see what I have gotten myself into this morning." Gently, I worked open the flap on the envelope treating it like a sacred text.

The letter written in red crayon read: "Dear Santa,"

I have been a very good little girl and I don't need anything for Christmas. But I do have some younger brothers. Troy needs a football, and Timmy needs a truck. I don't need anything for Christmas, but I do ask one favor. I have a tiny little brother named Tommy. He is very sick and is in St. Louis Children's Hospital. I would like to have him come home for Christmas. I have been very good.

Signed: Theresa Dennis – Age 8

"Ginny, did you tell her to give me the letter?" I challenged. "Why didn't you just tell them to leave it with the nurses? We know how to play Santa." She denied knowing anything about it. "Well, if you didn't know anything about it, then how did you know that it existed at all?" I told her thanks for calling me and that I was happy to help. I left knowing that we would be friends forever, although today I don't have any idea where she is or if she is still alive.

I had to put on the mind of Santa, but I really had to put on the mind of a student and prepare for pre-Christmas exams when I wasn't working at the hospital. This was my last year in the seminary. I had made it through eleven years starting with high school, and it wasn't the time to drop the ball. But that letter from Santa was seared into my psyche, and I had to come up with an answer.

I completed the exams at the seminary and went home for the holidays. I told my mom about the most pressing task that I had to complete before Christmas. Over the holidays, I had a job at the post office. With the burden of Christmas cards, the post office would hire extra letter carriers to make multiple residential deliveries. My mom said, "I will make some Santa Claus stationary for you and you think about what you are going to write to Theresa." She bought some card stock and cut out pictures from cards our family had received. On the top center of the card she pasted a picture of Santa and in calligraphy she wrote North Pole with a gold pen. On the right margin was a picture of Rudolph and on the left Santa's Sleigh. On the bottom was a Nativity scene.

After much prayer and pondering I wrote with the same gold pen:

> Dear Theresa,
>
> It is good to hear from you and old Santa knows that you are a very good little girl. I love you and all children very much. I am happy to give you the toys that you asked about for your brothers. Your unselfish spirit is what Christmas is all about – giving gifts to others. You know from your parents that your brother, Tommy, died in the hospital. While it is very hard, your unselfish gift at Christmas is to give Tommy back to God so that he can be with Jesus to celebrate at his birthday party in heaven.

I know that you understand because you know that
Christmas is all about GIVING.

I wish a very Merry Christmas to your whole family.

Santa

I sent the football and the truck for Theresa's brothers, and some
coloring books and crayons for Theresa who didn't need anything at all.

I didn't hear from the Dennis family again. I was tempted to visit
them, but I always had the fear that something might happen during the
visit that would reveal I was Jolly Old St. Nick.

In December 2010, forty-four years later, I received a message on
my voice mail. It was a stressed, teary voice that was difficult to understand. "Father Kleba, my name is Theresa Dennis. You don't know me,
but forty-four years ago you helped my family when my brother died. I
need to talk to you now, so please call me." With her sobbing, the message
was garbled and one of the numbers in the ten digits was muffled. However, I was determined to find her, so I dialed the number over and over
inserting one of the numbers from 0 – 9 until I got Theresa on the phone.
She was delighted when I called, and apologetic that she should take my
time. However, if she was delighted, I was euphoric that she remembered
me after forty-four years. If she was a tad bit happy; I was exuberant.

She began by apologizing, but I didn't allow her to get very far into
her apology before I interrupted. "Theresa, I know exactly who you are,
and I will tell you what I remember about you and your letter." I told her
the whole story, not without some tears on both ends of the phone. When
I was finished, I told her that I had often used her story as the heart of my
Christmas midnight mass homily. I sensed her disbelief, even though I
couldn't see her face.

Now it was her turn to talk. Theresa said, "My mother died last
year around Mother's Day. One of her last requests was that I should find
Father Kleba and tell him how important he has been in my family's life
every Christmas since Tommy's death. I told her that I would do this,
but I called some hospitals in St. Louis and no one knew who you were.

Then I was going through my mother's papers and I found a Christmas card that you wrote to us from Ste. Genevieve, MO in 1967. I called the church there and they told me where you are and gave me your phone number." She continued, "We always talked about you at Christmas, and since I became a teenager I always knew that you were our Santa Claus. About six years ago, our house burned down. I was standing in front of it watching the firemen fight the fire and I was saying, 'All of my precious things are burning up, my letter from Santa Claus.' My neighbors heard me say that, and they wondered what this forty-eight-year-old woman was saying about my letter from Santa Claus. I'm sure they thought I was in shock and talking nonsense because of the house fire."

I interrupted, "Theresa, your letter from Santa burned up, but I don't think that you need it anymore, because it is emblazoned on your mind and heart."

She thanked me and continued, "You have to know more about why this letter is so important to me. When Tommy died, I had some very strict Jehovah's Witnesses aunts and uncles. They said that since Tommy was not baptized, he went to Hell. They even said he went to Hell on the day of his funeral. I was so sad and scared that the only thing that brought me any consolation was re-reading my letter from Santa Claus and knowing that Tommy was celebrating at Jesus' birthday party in heaven." Now we were both in tears. "You don't know but maybe your letter saved an eight-year-old girl from committing suicide."

I couldn't believe my ears. How could I have done something that far back, forgotten it altogether, and yet still it had such a lasting impact on an entire family, especially on one very, very good little girl?

LETTER FROM THERESA (DENNIS) RAGSDALE

Jan. 3, 2011

Dear Father Kleba

Please forgive my tardiness in replying to your letter. Yes, I did receive the delicious chocolates, your book and picture. To me you are indeed the same handsome young man that touched my life so many years ago. As I opened your book and began to read I felt strangely connected. The date you signed the preface, May 1st, is my birthday.

These days are filled with me being a wife, mother and grandmother. Together my husband and I have three sons and eight grandchildren. My father, brothers and sisters all live in Davenport. My mother passed away May 13, 2009 from a long suffering battle with C.O.P.D. My father and I speak everyday on the phone. I also help him with housework several times a month.

I truly feel blessed to have found you after all of these years. I will always cherish your loving words and kindness. Thank you so very much for the consoling words you shared with my mother and father in their time of sorrow.

As I close this letter I am truly happy to know that our friendship will be a lasting one. You will always hold a special place in my heart and will always be my Santa Claus.

Sincerely,

Theresa (Dennis) Ragsdale

Sainte Genevieve Parish

"WELCOME TO STE. GENEVIEVE PARISH." That was the phone greeting I received from a priest, Father John Jadrick, whom I didn't know on the day after accepting my first assignment. He continued, "I know that you have a classmate assigned to the St. Louis Cathedral and others serving in wealthy suburban parishes and here you are assigned as the second assistant to a parish in the country. Well, I want to tell you that I served there as a young priest, and you are going to like it there and, besides that, I am going to pray for you."

That was the word I got even before I ever arrived in Ste. Genevieve Parish, in the historic town that was a bit of an art colony and a collection of French Colonial Upright Log houses. The Catholic faith there was as strong, deep and upright as the buildings in the town that had been settled in 1735 on the west bank of the mighty Mississippi.

When I arrived as the third priest in this parish of 1,800 families, the pastor, Msgr. Venverloh, studied me with his blue eyes and pink cherub face and laid out my assignments in a matter of fact, yet warm fashion.

"Father, as assistant here you will teach at Valle High School, visit the hospital two times a week, make Communion calls to the shut-ins, run the school cafeteria, moderate the Patron's Club, and celebrate weddings and funerals as they come along. Of course," he added, "you will say Mass every morning and several on Sundays. Now Father, that might sound like a lot of work to you, but remember always to have some fun too. Jesus said, 'The person who leaves everything to follow me will have a hundredfold in this life and life eternal.' You want to make sure you work hard enough, because you don't want to get more than your hundredfold and miss out on eternal life."

I assured him that I would want to be balanced and responsible, and I walked away from that meeting knowing that I wouldn't die of boredom.

25

"BE SHEPHERDS LIVING WITH THE SMELL OF THE SHEEP"

Pope Francis said, "We need to remember that all religious teaching ultimately has to be reflected in the teacher's way of life, which awakens the assent of the heart by its nearness, love and witness." Pope Francis. *Evangelii Gaudium – The Joy of the Gospel.* The Word Among Us Press. Frederick, Maryland. 2013. pp. 38-39.

The *Ste. Genvieve Herald* announced: **"Father Gerald Kleba Jaycee Distinguished Service Award Winner**

Father Gerald Kleba, assistant pastor at the Ste. Genevieve Catholic Church, was presented with the Distinguished Service Award. This award is annually presented to a young man between the ages of 21 and 35 who has demonstrated outstanding service to the community.

Mr. Gene Basler listed the many and varied humanitarian and civic services Father Kleba has initiated or participated in since his arrival nearly five years ago. Establishment of the Bargain Village on Merchant St. as a source of low-cost clothing for the low income and needy of the area and initiation of the movement for a county nursing home headed the list.

Summer visits to the impoverished area of Appalachia and the setting up of fund-raising projects for aid to the area were also cited by Mr. Basler. Enlisting the aid of youth in the Valle High School, wreaths and other items are made each Christmas and the profits forwarded to the Christian Appalachian Project. Under Father's supervision, toys and other items are also collected for distribution to the people of Appalachia. The initiation of an annual fund-raising campaign for the National Kidney Foundation was also added to Father's many activities.

Chairman Basler pointed out that Father Kleba is constantly seeking out opportunities to work toward the betterment of Ste. Genevieve. An

attack on the city dump issue that produced improvements and development of a program to secure low-income housing for the elderly of the
area were credited to Father Kleba by Mr. Basler.

Father's supervisory role in the shut-ins' retreat held four times
annually, his capable handling of the annual Patron's Club Variety Show
and many organizational and religious activities were pointed out by
Mr. Basler as well as his teaching duties at Valle High School. Basler's
commentary prior to the presentation concluded as follows: "He has
brought to the faithful of his church a new involvement in their religion,
and perhaps to many, a new understanding of their faith. In a way that
is uniquely his, he has the ability of making the individual a part of the
Sacrifice of the Mass he offers. . . and to bring all together in the love of
the Master he serves. This is his finest quality."

Betty Valle Gegg

January 27, 1972. Vol. 91, No 1. p. 1.

SUE LUTKEWITTE

"Peace I leave with you, peace is my great gift to you."

JOHN 14:27

ANY PASTOR KNOWS why the Sunday after Easter is called Low Sunday. Liturgists think that it refers to the lessened solemnity in comparison to the lavish brightness of the decorations and the triumphant Alleluias of Easter. But pastors know the real story. Low Sunday is called Low Sunday because the attendance is so low compared to Easter. Low Sunday was First Communion Sunday during my first year as a priest newly assigned to Ste. Genevieve Parish. First Communion put this Low Sunday into an entirely different category. The attendance at Mass was wall-bulging with the size of large rural families enhanced by the visiting grandparents, godparents, aunts and uncles. It was a challenging situation for me because it occurred a mere three weeks after my ordination. The pressure of this joyful celebration was heightened by the fact that the main Sunday Mass was broadcast weekly on KSGM Radio, which was EWTN for that time.

The gospel reading for the Sunday after Easter is the same every year. It is the story of Jesus appearing in the upper room, doubting Thomas questioning defiantly and then his great profession of faith, "My Lord and my God." Three times during these selected gospel verses Jesus says, "Peace be with you." As I considered my preaching at this important parish and family celebration, I decided that I would try to teach people, especially the first communicants, one of the words that Jesus certainly spoke. While there is much doubt and questioning about the "very words of Jesus," it is safe to say that Jesus used the word, "Abba" – Father, and the word "Shalom" – Peace. He used them quite frequently. I pondered how I could help the children understand this profound concept, Peace, and also teach them one of the words Jesus certainly spoke. That was the challenge.

I needed to teach them that peace was not a perpetual nap. Peace is not the absence of fighting with siblings or disobedience to parents and teachers. While these things are nice, peace is much more. Peace is a sense of inner quiet. Peace is a feeling of being raised up out of oneself. Peace is acceptance of the situation as it is and the world as it is. It is knowing that in every situation in which we live, God lives with us. And more, God is constantly giving us a big hug and surrounding us with love. I invited the children to give themselves a tight hug to remind themselves that God is present now and is present when they are alone and even when they are lonely.

God is with you there in your homes and with the people who are our family and friends. SHALOM! God is with you in school both during the hardest subject or at lunch and during recess with your friends. SHALOM! God is with you during summer vacation and when you are playing in or trudging through the snow and sledding down a hill. SHALOM! God is with you most closely on this First Communion day when you are surrounded by loved ones and when Jesus makes you strong with the Bread of Life. Since God is always with you even in your sleep or in the fears of night and the times of sickness you are a child of the Prince of Peace! SHALOM!

Then I concluded the sermon and asked, "Can anyone of you children tell me the word that Jesus spoke to say peace to his apostles in today's gospel story?" There was no response; in fact the church was so quiet that one could have heard a Kleenex drop on the shiny vinyl floor. Someone sneezed, and it felt like an earth tremor. I repeated, "I'm sure that one of you knows the word that Jesus used to say "peace." Who would like to tell me?" I could see a parent here and there nudging their shiny-faced, bright-eyed child, but no one responded. I wondered if I should call on the parent. Would the parent have enough courage to speak to the church crammed with 1,000 people? I waited and prayed silently feeling like a failure as a young preacher. I wondered whether this clever, little used audience participation scheme wasn't too far fetched. Either I was a failure because I had not communicated clearly or because I was so stupid as to try to have this question and answer period that had failed so miserably. I waited out the silence. In the second pew, right in front of the pulpit, was a family of nine, squeezed together shoulder to shoulder. A proud second grader stood up in her white dress. She had golden hair, a soft angelic face, powder puff pink cheeks and a strong, confident voice. She announced, "Jesus said Shalom" and it resonated up to the vaulted ceiling. My heart burst with love and I exhaled with relief since I had almost exploded holding my breath. A joyful smile lit up my face.

"Did all of you hear that, 'Jesus said Shalom?' Thank you, thank you very much. You answered so well and saved my homily. Let us proceed in the Peace of Christ."

I continued with Mass, but I could hardly wait to finish and finally meet this lifesaver girl and the family in the second pew. They were first rate in my mind. I would learn during my next six years in the parish that this family practically owned the second pew for the Mass that was broadcast on the radio. In fact, in colonial days throughout the eighteenth century, Ste. Genevieve Church had a New Year's Day auction of the best pews in church. This gave the buyers the right to tell intruders to exit their purchased pew. That was no longer the case, but if possession is nine-tenths of the law, the Lutkewitte's could have been equally demanding in the mid-twentieth century.

After Mass, I finished visiting with other First Communion families before approaching the family waiting on the church porch in the shadows of the massive gothic doors. It was the family of the glowing, clear-voiced girl who saved my homily. Her name was Mary Sue, and she was the youngest of seven children of Joe and Rosemary Lutkewitte. They were a prominent family in the community, because Joe was one of three medical doctors in the town. It took little time for me to determine that this family would become one that I would know well and become closely attached to. They were proud and warm-hearted on that special family day and displayed such a luminous joy it was no wonder that Mary Sue's angelic look was part of the Lutkewitte illumination. They were equally delighted to meet me, the new priest in town.

Mary Sue's eyes met mine as I crouched down and looked into her dazzling face and commended her for saving my homily and ego with her clear confident statement. "You saved my life, because I was dying with the long dead silence and wondered whether anyone had learned the word, Shalom." I gave her a hug and promised that I would come to their home in the afternoon for their First Communion party. The entire family, including the older siblings, Carolyn, Mary Ann, Kathy, Joe, Rosemary and Karl was there. I was thrilled by their general sense of warm hospitality and profound reverence they had for priests. They were proud of their Catholic faith. Parents Joe and Rosemary were delighted in celebrating this most important sacrament with their "baby." It was obvious this was a family that knew shalom in their lives. They also knew how to radiate it to others. It only took a few months for me to develop a close relationship with them, one that I have maintained even after leaving St. Genevieve.

One of my assignments in this parish was to be the chaplain at the Ste. Genevieve County Memorial Hospital. In the days before cell phones and answering machines, this was a very demanding assignment each weekend. I had to stay at the rectory on constant call in anticipation that an emergency might arise. This was very lonely and tedious as the other priests in the parish always found something to do on Sundays, leaving me alone to wait for a phone call from the hospital. It was impossible for me to even go for a walk because I couldn't be away from the hotline. After a few weeks of boredom, I was seething at the injustice of this particular task and thought that this could lead to depression or alcoholism. If those things didn't kill me, I could die of boredom.

One day while mulling over the situation, I remembered that Dr. Lutkewitte had a lake house where their family escaped every weekend. The lake house was blessed with a phone line. The hospital would be able to reach me whenever they had an emergency. I asked the Lutkewitte's if I could spend my Sunday's with them. Then, should the hospital have an emergency, it could call and get a priest and a doctor all for the price of one phone call. The family eagerly welcomed me and wondered why they had not thought of it themselves. However, the truth was that the hospital was brand new and so the concern was new also.

Thus began a long and happy relationship that drew me closer to the Lutkewitte's and preserved my sanity and perseverance as a parish priest. It taught me much about marriage and family life as I greatly admired Joe and Rosemary's relationship. This included Rosemary's single parenting demands when Joe was working long hours or leaving in the middle of the night for some emergency or birth. Add to that, their joyful respect for and pride in their children's every accomplishment. I was always welcome at the lake and sometimes my absence was questioned if I missed for several weeks. I would swim with the kids, play cards or Monopoly when the weather was bad and enjoy eating Doc's barbeque as much as he enjoyed preparing it. I helped to set the table and sometimes helped with the dishes. Over my six years in the parish, I ate hundreds of meals with the "L. Family" and I always knew that Mary Sue's "shalom" opened the door.

When I left Ste. Genevieve in 1973 for my next assignment, Mary Sue was in eighth grade. It was hard to forfeit this rural, Catholic utopia for Visitation, an inner-city parish, facing the challenges of poverty and urban abandonment. The rolling river hills were lush, verdant, serene and life-giving; while the city provided many overgrown lots, littered streets and decrepit vacant buildings. It felt life threatening. Beyond that, I had to face my own racism and that of a larger society in a historically segregated city. St. Louis was the largest city in the state of Missouri, a slave state that had never left the union during the Civil War. Consequently it suffered from a social schizophrenia. Additionally, it was heart-wrenching to leave the Sunday Lutkewitte gatherings.

Frequently, I returned to the many Sunday gatherings at the lake and sometimes brought Protestant minister friends along with me for a swim and dinner. Sometimes Mom and Dad L. would invite them to say the blessing before dinner. Mom and Dad L. was the signature I always saw on postcards I received when they wrote me from their vacation destinations. The cards were addressed, "Dear Son Gerry." The added blessing, when

I visited from the city, was that I was welcome to stay overnight. When they built a fancier vacation home on a larger lake, I stayed overnight there before any other member of the family.

Four years after joining my city parish, I was called by the Cenacle Retreat House to preach a retreat for some high school seniors. I agreed to do that and found on arrival that the class gathered there were the senior girls from Valle, the Catholic high school, in Ste. Genevieve Parish. Mary Sue was one of the students in that class and it was a joy to recall so much of life that we had shared since her First Communion. When I was bidding the class farewell at the end of the retreat, Mary Sue took me aside after the others had headed for the school bus. She told me that when she was sixteen and got her driver's license her dad gave her car keys on a ring with a brass medallion embossed *Shalom*. Each letter was painted in different colored enamels. She showed it to me with a giddy smile and then gave it to me. "I want to give this to you. Shalom."

I hugged her and was almost in tears, humbled that she would remember this ancient event. I whispered "Shalom" in her ear as I was filled with a spirit of peace. Peace is not a nap, but an alert awareness of the blessed present.

More years went by. During that time, I spent fewer Sundays with the Lutkewitte's but continued to enjoy our contacts and never felt unwelcome even if I barged in unannounced. Since my Ste. Genevieve days, I had celebrated several Lutkewitte weddings and Mary Sue had become simply Sue. In 1991, Sue got married to Tim McDonough. I returned the *Shalom* medallion as a wedding present. Some of the enamel had worn off with contact from my car keys. "May Shalom and happiness permeate all your years of married life," I wrote on the wedding card.

If I had stayed home all those Sundays many years earlier waiting for phone calls from the hospital, I would have died of boredom or lived with bitterness. I would have had personal quiet but no inner peace. I would have been pitiful and angry; not shalom filled. No Sunday calls from the hospital ever came, and no one ever died. In the process, I was becoming more vibrant sharing life and meals with the Lutkewitte's. The meal, a weekly banquet, was frequently Doc's barbeque and Rosemary's home cookin' with the family gathered around a long table. In 1967, on that First Communion Sunday, Sue announced to a crowded church, "Jesus said Shalom." Surrounded by Sue and her entire family Jesus certainly gave "Shalom" to me.

FROM SUE LUTKEWITTE, 8/8/12

> I am deeply touched that you felt so close to us all. I so often reflect on those wonderful times at the lake with us all. Our family was so blessed and still is blessed with the wonderful peace our parents gave us.
> — Love Sue, Shalom

❖

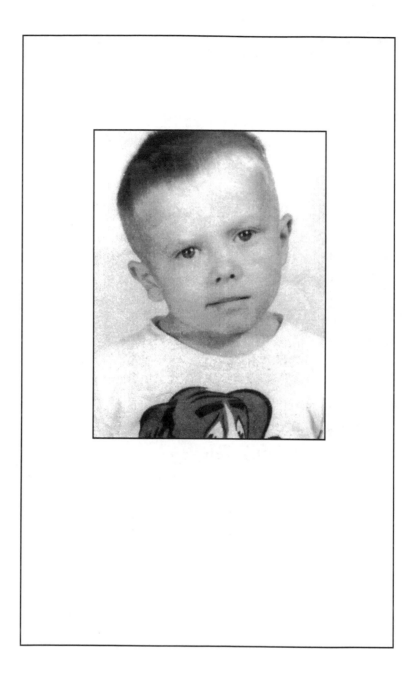

GARI LaHAY

"As life quickens by and the generations pass, stories are handed down like heirlooms, told and retold to help us try to make sense of it all."

Mark Phillips

MY FIRST PASTORAL ASSIGNMENT was in Ste. Genevieve, Missouri, a charming French settlement (1735) along the Mississippi River. It was founded by "let the good times roll" French from New Orleans, but with the disappearance of slavery, many hardworking Germans settled there. My pastor told me that the best epitaph on the tombstone of a German farmer would be, "He worked hard and he saved." With both French and German influences, the faith life was as deeply rooted in Catholicism as the pecan trees were rooted in the rich river bottom-land called "Le Grand Champ," the Big Field. This town with a population of 5,000 could have been called Lake Wobegon, Missouri because it was a living anachronism.

If the certainties in the wider world are death and taxes, the certainties in Ste. Genevieve are the Catholic Church and Valle High School Football. The Warriors were the winning-est team in Missouri State High School athletics at the time. The Valle High School football team had won all of its games. Along with being undefeated, as unbelievable as it sounds, none of the opponents scored a single point. Valle's varsity totaled 679 points and the ten opposing teams eked out zero on the gridiron. The coach, Ralph Thomure, believed in excellence and hard work, and the players bought into the program. The community boasted Ste. Genevieve Catholic Church, with its grade school and high school as the religious center of the community. Along with the sacramental duties in this parish of 1,700 families, I was also expected to be the hospital chaplain and a religion instructor in the grade school and high school.

New priests in the community were notable commodities and I was noticed for the fact that I didn't drive the newest car on the showroom floor. In fact, while I was the youngest member of my ordination class, I owned the oldest car. I arrived in 1967 driving a 1955 Chevy two-door with stick shift, two-tone, green on the bottom with a white roof. I was the talk of the town and the gossip of teenagers over the ordinariness of this quaint little car. In an era when the car culture in the United States was flourishing, no teenagers told me to "pop the hood and let's see what makes this puppy run." I considered it a rainbow on wheels and Gari LaHay called it the Bill Haley mobile, "shake, rattle, and roll."

Kids scoffed at it, and since the parish rectory was on the town square by the county courthouse, everyone saw the car parked in the priests' garage. Priests in Ste. Genevieve were cherished like the village Pope, but my shabby car was seriously undercutting the height of the pedestal on which folks would place me. This was a running joke with the high school students who didn't think I was cool or hot or groovy or whatever was the positive descriptive for a small town celebrity at that time.

My car even became the topic of discussion at a Knights of Columbus Meeting where a German parish patriarch noted the lack of respect that my car and I endured. With a heavy accent he commented, "I ust don't tink it's right the way dese high skuul kits make fun of Fader Klebe's car. Day ought to show more proper respect for de priest's car. Now dat's dat." In Ste. Genevieve elder talk about important issues was not debatable and that's that.

There were lots of sports celebrities at Valle when I arrived in Ste. Genevieve that victorious year, but there was a non-athletic, frail boy who caught my attention early on. His name was Gari LaHay, and he was in eighth grade. He was living with a debilitating disease called syringomyelea. He was hardly able to walk even with crutches. He had a marvelous sense of humor and like most quick witted folk was not intellectually short changed. Gari teased almost anyone; it was something of an achievement to be included on his list. He would never bully anyone. He was so funny that he even got away with his antics with the no-nonsense, six-foot tall nun who taught eighth grade, Sister Baptista. Baptista was a sister who wore the traditional nun's habit with the rosary at her side. She was at home with a spirited bunch of students who found extra energy rallying around Gari LaHay, a boy with obvious disabilities. While he might have been physically less able than his classmates, many of whom were exceptional athletes, he had a sense of humor that always kept him the center of things, oftentimes the center of mischief. While Gari was mobility-challenged, he drew the long straw when it came to his bedevilment quotient. He was like another Missouri native son, Tom Sawyer, who was able to convince others to do his bidding and feel proud of their accomplishments in the process. Tom succeeded getting others to whitewash his fences, while Gari egged classmates on to other trickery especially regarding my trusted Chevy.

Whatever might have been the prevailing thinking at the Knights of Columbus meeting or the authority of a parish patriarch, Gari saw nothing wrong with undermining the new priest by literally undermining "Fader Klebe's" car. Gari got his trusted henchmen to tie six tin cans to the frame under my car while it was parked in the garage. I backed the car out of the garage and it sounded like the loser in the demolition derby as I drove down the street. While it sounded like the innards had fallen out of the car, I proceeded down the street anyway. I noticed that the rascals were camped on a park bench across the street from the rectory, so I was not about to express any upset. I kept driving the clunker and waved to them and honked as I drove.

While it was customary for the three priests at the parish to leave the garage doors open throughout the day to accommodate our frequent comings and goings, some of Gari's classmates decided that it would be good to close my garage door whenever my car was in so that my $300.00 investment wouldn't be an embarrassment to the priests and make us look second class in comparison to the Protestant ministers in town. Willie Hoffmann's car cemetery and huge junkyard was down the street near the river. Gari would have notes pasted on my car window suggesting that my car get a proper funeral amidst the other rotting wrecks.

Gari was the son of Walt and Delores LaHay. He had two sisters, Lynette and Laura Louise. Lyn was the eldest and a fine pianist. Laura Louise, affectionately nicknamed Weezie, played the guitar. Weezie was a very innocuous nickname by Ste. Genevieve standards. In fact, nicknames were so common that people were listed by their nickname in the phone book. Long time residents often didn't even know a relative's baptismal name. Some of the tamer nicknames were Izzie, Dizzy, Nuts, Hammer, Boots, and an undertaker named Punkin. There were some borderline calls with folks sporting monikers like Piss Ant and Chicken Shit.

There was a family with the last name of Sexauer. One of the family members appeared on the 1960s television quiz show "You Bet Your Life" hosted by Groucho Marx. Groucho used the entire half hour making jokes about the contestant's last name and never got around to asking one of the quiz questions. He gave him the big prize of $500.00. Town lore also recounts the time the human resource office at the town's largest employer, Mississippi Lime Company, received a call from the Department of Labor. The caller asked, "Do you have a Sexauer there?" The fitting, albeit snarky reply was, "Sex hour— hell we don't even have a coffee break."

The entire LaHay family were staunch, respected members of the community and diligent in their care of Gari. After Gari entered high school, he became sicker, his absences became more frequent, and his trips to the hospital in St. Louis required longer stays. Throughout all of this, his parents spoke in glowing terms about Gari's doctor, Henry Lattinville. Sometimes I would visit Gari at DePaul Hospital in St. Louis. This was quite a trek, so I usually did it when I was in St. Louis visiting my family on a day off. The trip was about eighty miles one way, much of it on two lane curvy hills without paved shoulders. It was the first time that I ever visited a child in isolation and under an oxygen tent.

However, those visits were infrequent in comparison to the times when I would visit Gari at home in the evenings. Getting to know the family was made easier because I was frequently accompanied by the other associate pastor. His name was Ken Zimmermann. He was only a few years older than me. We had been friends in the seminary and immediately hit it off as co-conspirators by introducing the reforms of Vatican II to this parish that was staid and tradition-bound.

Since Gari's two sisters were both quite musical, a visit to the LaHay home was often a musical recital with Laura playing the piano and Louise strumming the guitar. There were a lot of laughs during those visits. Since I was the new priest in town, Walt LaHay, who, as a gas company repairman, knew everyone, and would fill me in on all the stories and characters that made the Ste. Genevieve landscape so colorful. He knew where all the bodies were buried.

All of these things were important background information for me as a new priest who was trying to get established in this cozy community. Historians say there are fifty upright log homes from the pre-Civil War era. Many of those homes are from the French colonial days. A number of these historic homes are now hidden under layers of vinyl siding and weathered wooden shake shingles. Not only did the church steeple tower over the town, but the Catholic presence was even more dominant.

Throughout all of the music and conversation during the visits to the LaHay home, Gari was never out of the picture. While his voice was not too melodic, instead squawky, his humor made the music of laughter melt into the instrumentation. The home was joyful. I was eagerly welcomed into the LaHay circle in a town where newcomers were still considered outsiders often into their third generation.

Gari had more operations and became more stiff and disabled. Once during the summer, Ken Zimmermann and I organized a backyard Mass and celebration with his classmates at Gari's house. The Mass was followed by a picnic. During the fall of his sophomore year, Gari went to football games in a wheelchair. His Valle High School spirit never waned, and his presence at the games was important. In the category of off the field courage and strength of spirit, Gari was an Olympian. In the locker room, several of the Valle victories were dedicated to Gari. The school had a great football tradition and looked for inspiration wherever it was to be had. Gari was energy and determination.

Gari died during my third year at the parish. Nobody involved in seminary preparation spent any time helping the future priest learn how to be with a dying child and his inconsolable family members. I really don't know how well I performed in any of those roles, but I do know that I concelebrated Gari's funeral Mass with Ken Zimmermann. It was devastating for all of those loving classmates who developed new bonds and a stronger relationship because of Gari.

Now, years later, when I am with some of Gari's friends and former classmates, his name still gets mentioned. Stories are remembered and all of them are sprinkled with a kind of "cat is out of the bag" twitter. It's always a "remember when" moment. When Sister Baptista's name is thrown into the mix, someone is sure to say, "She always liked the boys more." And they would be right.

At a party after the funeral, there was a reading of the will. I don't think a fortune was distributed that day, but I do know it was the first will that mentioned my name. I was present during the reading of the will and discovered I was to receive some of Gari's prized possessions, two joke books. For me, that young man was a shining example of the human spirit.

Twenty-five years later, I was serving at St. Joseph Parish in Clayton, Missouri. After Mass one Sunday, a gentleman resembling Spencer Tracy with thick, wavy gray hair and a Brooks Brothers flair stopped to visit me. He complimented me on my homily and I asked his name.

"I'm Henry Lattinville," he responded in a genteel and melodious voice.

"Are you "the" Dr. Henry Lattinville," I inquired?

With a humble smile and a twinkle, he replied, "I don't know whether I am "The" Dr. Henry Lattinville, but I am Dr. Henry Lattinville."

"Doctor, I've never met you, but you were canonized by friends of mine who were ardent admirers of yours twenty-five years ago."

"I was? And who might they be?"

"There was a boy in Ste. Genevieve when I was a young priest, and his name was Gari LaHay. He died when he was a sophomore in high school, and his parents always spoke about you with such respect and gratitude. You were the incarnation of the Hippocratic Oath to them. It is really a pleasure to meet you, and I appreciate your kind words to me even more now that I know who you are."

Doctor Lattinville responded, and I was amazed that a neurosurgeon had such total recall about a patient who had died years back. I thought that many lesser doctors wouldn't remember any of their patients from the old days, but would be quick to forget one who had died. After all, wasn't that a failure?

"Gari was the gutsiest and most courageous boy I ever met. One time his dad brought him up to my office and when it was his appointment time, he made me come out to the parking lot to see Gari ride his bicycle. I just couldn't believe it. That boy was never supposed to walk and here he was riding a bike. It was amazing."

We parted that day, but I knew that I wanted to speak with Henry and his wife, Marie, again. I didn't know it would be so soon. Two days later at 5:00 p.m., Henry Lattinville was at the rectory door. He said, "Since you mentioned Gari LaHay, I went to my file and got out some of my notes so I could recall the story about that fine lad. Do you know that his parents still have the same phone number? I called their home this afternoon and told them about our conversation. I thanked them for remembering me so fondly. Do you know that Walt is retired and Delores is still working in the nursery at the Ste. Genevieve County Memorial Hospital? It was just wonderful talking to them."

Since Dr. Lattinville had already been canonized, I knew that was one job I wouldn't have to tackle. LaHay and Lattinville would be in alphabetical order in the Book of Life. Until my name joins them on that list, I have my joke books from Gari LaHay.

FROM GARI'S SISTER, LAURA

Good to hear from you. What an endeavor, taking on the memories of relationships over the course of your career! ... I am thankful every day that we can all depend on each other and, although some aspects of re-establishing ties with all members of the family have not worked out so well, I am reminded of the things that are truly important through the small trials of prioritizing in relationships.

Take care, Laura

❖

Visitation Parish

IN THE SUMMER OF 1973, I asked Cardinal Carberry if I could leave St. Louis and serve the church in a remote area of Appalachia in Eastern Kentucky. He denied my request and asked me to serve the poor by going to Visitation Parish in the black community of North St. Louis. (I wrote about this in *THE PEOPLE PARISH, A Model of Church Where People Flourish*.)

There was a great sense of black pride and ownership in that parish. A visionary pastor had integrated the school in 1946, eight years before the Supreme Court decision, Brown vs. the Board of Education. The decision stated, "Separate, but equal is not equal." There was a "hold your head up high" pride exhibited by many of the people at Visitation.

I struggled with my own racism at Visitation, I was frequently the only white face in the crowd and sometimes overwhelmed by the fear of violence in the black community. Racism is as much a part of the fabric of American life as pollution in the air, fluoride in the water and humidity in a St. Louis summer. I could not deny it, and it was part of my shadow side that came to light. I had to heal it by lovingly listening at Visitation, a parish that was small, personal and vibrant.

"BE SHEPHERDS LIVING WITH THE SMELL OF THE SHEEP"

Pope Francis said, "Any Church community, if it thinks it can comfortably go its own way without creative concern and effective cooperation in helping the poor to live with dignity and reaching out to everyone, will also risk breaking down, however much it may talk about social issues or criticize governments. It will easily drift into a spiritual worldliness camouflaged by religious practices, unproductive meetings and empty talk." Ibid. *Evangelii Gaudium.* pp. 150-51.

In the *National Catholic Reporter* Bill Kenkelen wrote in *Reporter at large*: "ST. LOUIS, MO. –- Visitation Parish in North St. Louis is an upbeat story in a beat up area. The pastor, Father Gerry Kleba, says the parish is trying to learn how to take care of its own. North St. Louis is just one more replay of U.S. urban blues: what whites and businesses fled is now a black refuge.

The brocade and velvet of "Meet Me in St. Louis" (the song originated in this area), is second-hand polyester and worn denim. Delicate, ornamental brick architecture built before 1904 when the World's Fair was held near here still stands. The brick is strong, but the cement around it crumbles; the wood frame windows disintegrate and rot; inside linoleum cracks.

The odds against Visitation parish have been high. Most Catholics have left the area for the suburbs. Visitation has only about 400 active parishioners in an area with approximately 16,000 people. The parish has a vision: it aims to reach and help the entire community.

Next to Andy Wurm's Tire Co. on Martin Luther King Drive is the office of the Visitation Community Credit Union. It is the keystone of the parish's nuts and bolts efforts to shore up economic life in the neighborhood.

The parish recently began a home repair service. With government monies, it provides jobs for youths. They primarily help older residents rehabilitate their homes.

Even though the parish barely manages to stay financially afloat, Kleba said parishioners managed to give away thousands of dollars last year. "The whole meaning of church would be lost," said Kleba, "if you're not constantly doing what you can for those less fortunate than you."

Kleba quickly brushes aside criticism that says the church shouldn't be deeply involved in the struggle for social change. He points to this 1971 Synod of Bishops statement: "Action on behalf of justice and participation in the transformation of the world appear to us as a constitutive dimension of the preaching of the gospel." Only by deep involvement in community life can the church be an effective force, and even survive, in the ghetto, Kleba claims."

April 28, 1978. pp. 4-5.

MEV PULEO

I HAD JUST BARELY SETTLED IN AT VISITATION, my new parish, in the heart of the African-American community of St. Louis. To say "settled in" means that I had unpacked my boxes, put my clothes in the closet and books on the shelves. My sheltered life in white middle class America had been jolted every step of the way with the transfer to this traditional black community on the impoverished north side of the city. I had grown up in lily white south St. Louis. I had gone to the seminary for twelve years beginning with high school. There was only one black student in my class of about one hundred.

After ordination, I was stationed in Ste. Genevieve, Missouri where only a dozen blacks lived in a town of 5,000. These were the few who remained after the race riot of 1930, which had resulted in the departure of most blacks. Most of these blacks were either employed by a prominent Ste. Genevieve family with deep roots in the 250-year-old settlement, or by the town's Catholic church. The patriarch of this prominent family was the sacristan and valet to the Catholic church's pastor. The local pastor for 54 years, Msgr. Charles A. VanTurenhaut, was widely regarded as the village Pope. There were still signs on the rear pillars on both sides of the church proclaiming "Negroes behind these signs." Those signs were removed three decades after the race riot. The priest who was pastor during my time of service there instructed me, "If I am on vacation and some member of a black family dies and wants to have the funeral here, serve them the best that you know how, even if you have never seen them in church. How could anyone feel at home in this church after such hateful treatment?"

My transfer to the inner city of St. Louis meant that the racial cards were totally reshuffled. I was the only white person in a mile radius and that was quite intimidating. It was the mid-seventies and St. Louis had avoided the riots, burnings and lootings that plagued other cities with large black populations. Some people credited that peacefulness to the presence of Msgr. John Shocklee, the pastor of the largest black parish, which was also located in the housing projects. If it was true that Shocklee deserved credit, then I was proud to be a priest riding on his coattails.

Upon my arrival, I was flattered to receive a phone call from a sister who ran the religion department at Visitation Academy. While this school and our parish had the same name, that is where all similarity ended. Our parish is as I have already described, but the school was an all white, all-girls school in the wealthy part of St. Louis suburbia. Sister asked, "Would you be interested in coming out to Visitation Academy and giving a day of recollection to the girls?"

That was a simple request, and it came to me at a time when I was befuddled regarding my responsibilities at this new parish. I did have some experience teaching religion and heading student mission trips at the all white Valle High School in my former parish in Ste. Genevieve. My pastor at Visitation Parish was a recluse and was extremely non-directive, almost non-communicative. I was inclined to accept the invitation and maybe have a taste of success in this new and chaotic situation. My fears and unacknowledged racism were deeply perplexing. I asked, "Sister, what would be the theme of the day and who would plan the schedule and the various activities?" I admitted, "This would be a new experience for me. I have to tell you I'm curious about why you even thought of me as a presenter at your school in the first place?"

"Well I have seen you at some of the charismatic prayer meetings on Saturday nights at our school and so I thought that we would ask you since you would be a new face for us."

Now that I had a few minutes to think, getting over the surprise of the call, I thought that I would hit her with a novel idea that would certainly tell me how truly eager they were to have me. "Sister, here is my proposal for you. If you and some of the girls on the planning committee want to come into the heart of the city at Visitation East, then I will come out to your high school, Visitation west. What do you think of that? See if you can find some girls who are open to coming and see if their parents will allow them to come into the 'hood'."

She told me that was a fair offer and that she would call back in a couple of days and give me an answer. I didn't know if I was hoping for a positive answer because it would help me to get out of this nerve-wracking situation. Or perhaps I was looking for a negative response so that I could dig in a bit, find some local needs and address my own racism. Whatever I was wishing, Sister called back the very next evening and told me that there were students who were open to my challenge. They were ready to come into the city. When I came to my senses I said to myself, "This assignment is certainly stretching me, so I ought to stretch others."

Sister arrived with five students at the agreed-upon time and they plunked themselves down on the floor of my office. They dressed in their Christmas red Visitation Academy uniform jumpers hemmed just above the knee with white blouses and bobby socks. Their brown shoes with leather tongues that folded over the laces on the top of the shoes. The girls were bubbly and excited and told me this was their first time in this area of the city. They noted how dilapidated, poor, and bombed out it appeared to be. They were giddy about this adventure outside of their comfort zone. I was sure that many of the girls had garages or swimming pools that were bigger than the houses in our community. Since that was their experience just in the drive through the neighborhood, we toyed with putting together a day that would focus on an experience of poverty. We would have some presentations and booths staffed by people from a homeless shelter and a soup kitchen. We would end the day with a Mass praying that all people realize their unity in creation and oneness in the People of God. This was complex and took several planning meetings, because I had little experience with local poverty myself.

It didn't take me long to discover one particular girl, Mev Puleo, who was notable for her warmth, energy, enthusiasm and ideas. Her energy and smile could light up the sky on a sunny day. She exuded a bouncy joy even when sitting on the floor in a cross-legged yoga position. Mev

was the daughter of Pete and Evelyn Mae Puleo. The family lived in La-
due, an upscale St. Louis suburb. Her dad, Pete, had grown up in Msgr.
Shocklee's parish. He served Mass for him and viewed him as a Super-
man for his courage and integrity in inner-city ministry. So Mev had a
greater experience of diversity at the local level. Her international travel
experiences had also given her a bigger picture of the world than her more
sheltered classmates. I only discovered these things later as I got to know
her better and became a bit of a fixture at Visitation Academy. Mev came
with many ideas and the networking skills to put people together when
these ideas called for broad-based participation.

The big idea for that Day of Recollection revolved around helping
the students understand the plight of the hungry. Mev explained, "This is
the way we will do it. We will cancel the school food service for that day
and tell all the girls that they are to pack their own lunch. But in a spirit
of sharing, we will tell them that they are not going to eat the lunch they
bring. They are to bring the lunch to the gym in the morning and put it
on one of the numbered seats on the bleachers. Then, they are to pick a
number off of one of the other seats where someone else's lunch is placed.
At lunch time, they will get a lunch other than their own." These ideas
didn't roll out in one breath or in one meeting, but they developed out of
the shared wisdom of the gathering.

"When lunch time comes, everyone will be thinking they will
get a lunch that one of the other girls has brought. But at lunchtime,
we will have the cafeteria staff collect the tickets and bring lunches to
the classrooms. They will come with one bag containing a Big Mac and
fries and a malted milk, two of the brown bag lunches and the rest of the
students will get a cup of cold water and a slice of white bread. When
the meals are distributed, there will be an outcry about the uneven
distribution of the food. It will be up to the teacher to get a dialogue
going about the rich and poor of the world and the responsibility the
well-off have to share their abundance."

Another girl was having an 'aha' moment and chimed in, "It's all as
random as the birth lottery. No one has a say as to where they are born;

what country, what family, what race. It's just the way it happens, no vote and no questions asked.

"WOW," everyone was impressed with the idea, but wondering about how angry people would be about not getting the lunch that they had been promised.

Mev had a follow-up plan for that. "When students are irate about this horrible situation, the teacher can tell them that if they are still hungry, they can go to the gym and claim one of the undistributed lunches. When the girls get to the gym, they would see that we fixed it up with desks and a waiting area like a welfare office. The sisters and teachers would be the case workers. Students would fill out a form to prove they are poor enough, financially eligible and truly needy and hungry enough to get a meal. Once everybody settled down, we would gather together to celebrate Mass and conclude the day."

"If they ever settle down, we will have Mass," I interjected with doubt in my voice. It was to be my job to settle them down and lead a meaningful celebration.

Everybody was excited, and I was amazed at the spirit and the social conscience of the students who volunteered for this special day. Not only had the students come to Visitation East as I had suggested, but they came with an awareness that had roots deeper than could have developed in this first trip to the black ghetto. Now it was up to me to organize the various ministries, prepare my talk and the homily for the Mass. In two weeks, I would be off to Visitation West.

When the day came, students arrived cheerily with their brown bags in hand looking forward to the adventure of sharing a surprise lunch rather than the limited and predictable cafeteria menu. Dutifully, they turned in their lunches and were each given a number of the brown bag lunch they would get at noon. The morning talk went well, and people also made small group presentations. Some were from the Catholic Worker House, St. Patrick's Homeless Center, Meals on Wheels, and the Salvation Army Detox Center called Harbor Light. Soon it was lunchtime, and the meal carts arrived outside the classrooms. Deliveries were made and wide-eyed girls, who were usually as mannerly as convent school girls should be, reacted with annoyed disbelief. The winner couldn't believe her luck at scoring the Big Mac lunch, but the losers were not at all humored by their humble meal of bread and water. The remaining girls were given the brown bags just as they had expected, but they were distracted from their own abundance by the paltry pickings given to the group that was fast becoming an angry mob. The teacher tried to silence the uproar, but that was like quieting a rock concert. These girls were mad.

The teacher asked over the uproar, "What do we see here, and what can we learn from this experience today?" The question was to no avail. No one heard it and even if they did it was not a teachable moment.

"We learned that we don't pay this much tuition to come to this school so that we can starve to death," was one haughty reply screeched over the din. With that, several of the girls took their bread and water and tossed it in the trash, making as much racket as possible. Teachers who had agreed to this program hesitantly now questioned their own sanity and gathered to talk and strategize out in the hall. They encouraged each other to hang in there patiently and remind students that this is a day of recollection. "See if someone has a courageous insight to share or has a conscientious moment of awareness," one offered hopefully. "I hoped this would be more transformative with more to ponder and less to protest." They returned to the battle zones that were their homerooms. In one classroom the anger had settled a bit, and the teacher asked the question about meaning once more.

Someone volunteered, "We see the unequal distribution of wealth and food in the world." She might have been one of the plants from the planning committee, since this hubbub was predicted and needed to be directed.

One of the girls who had more food, took half of her sandwich and half of an apple to share with another. One was grateful, and one retorted shouting, "I don't need any of your charity, I was supposed to get a lunch of my own."

After a while, when the carping somewhat subsided but with a remaining undercurrent of boiling anger, the teacher made an announcement. "We hope that you have learned something here. In a spirit of solidarity with the poor of the world, you will suffer a bit of hunger, and at the end of the school day, have an opportunity to eat one of the lunches."

This was not enough to offer those who were seething, and who had learned only more hard heartedness through this routine. The teacher continued, "If it is impossible for you to wait until after school and your stomach is growling so much that starvation is imminent, you can go down to the gym now and get a lunch." With that, half of the students rushed eagerly into the hall and down the steps to the gym. The shoving and elbowing looked like Roller Derby maneuvers.

Since the early morning, efforts had been made to transform the gym into a welfare office with sisters and teachers staffing the desks. It would not be a simple process of turning in your number and getting some food if you said that you were hungry. Instead, you had to wait until your number was called. Sister would then give the student a questionnaire to fill out rather than simply hand over a brown bag lunch. The students were outraged to get another piece of paper, but they were even more infuriated to read the questions. "What difference does it make what kind of car I drive?" one girl screamed, waving the paper with rage.

"Who cares what credit cards I have?" was the shout of a girl as she crumpled up the form and threw it at the nun. Some attempted to steal a lunch from the bleachers. The thieves then had to face the janitor dressed as a security guard. The scene was mayhem. I knew it was going to be quite a challenge to bring the girls together for the Eucharist.

Before the prayer time started, one of the senior planners came to the front of the gym in an attempt to instill peace and unity in the very place where violence and shouting had prevailed moments before. She addressed the girls, thanking them for their participation and beseeching them to ponder the injustice and inequity of our world as we ask God's blessing on all of us, rich and poor alike. It was a challenge to get stillness for the quiet time and get the girls singing at the song time. It was hard to

ignore that something profound had been experienced that day. At the
end of the day, girls were reminded that there were still brown bags for
those who wanted them, but many were still so angry or awed by the in-
tensity of the day's events that they went home empty handed. I believe,
since I still receive comments years later from these former students, they
left school having had an unforgettable experience. To this day, they have
an awareness of the social gospel engendered by that small exercise in
hunger. I wondered whether I would ever be invited back to Visitation
Academy after that day, but I was invited back several times.

Another time the girls came to Visitation East was to prepare for the
day of recollection on November 2nd, All Souls Day. We would celebrate it
with the theme, "Today Is the Last Day of Your Life." When I was preparing
my talks and reviewing the schedule on the preceding day, All Saints Day, I
questioned how it was that I could participate in this day. If I were to
present this theme, I had to get into the mindset, and I just wasn't there.
I had to really believe that this was the last day of my lie, because I don't
have a good poker face. I just couldn't bluff my way through it.

I asked myself, "If this were really the last day of your life, would
you spend it at a girls' high school in upscale suburbia?" I had anticipated
that I would spend it with my eighty-year-old mother. "If this were the last
day of your life, would you go to a school where students have Saks Fifth
Avenue credit cards in their wallets?"

"If this were the last day of your life, would you drive your car once
more and pollute the environment?"

Once I had the answers to all those questions, I decided I could do
it. I would keep my promise to be there with girls whom I didn't know
well except for Mev, who had once invited me to dinner at her home. I
decided I would ride my bike to the school about twenty miles away. I
would not pollute the planet, in fact, I would leave early enough to stop
at the Forest Park Zoo on my ride. For me it would parallel Adam and
Eve's first day in paradise: my last day being spent at the zoo. Well, I asked
myself, "What should I wear to ride my bike to a fancy school? If I arrive
all sweaty, what will these girls think?"

I decided that the most important question I had to answer was, "What do I care? It's the last day of my life, so I can do whatever I think is right. I don't care what you think because I'm never going to see you again." That was the key, I don't care about your opinion because, "After today I'm out of here, so you can take it or leave it. I've got this one last day and I am gonna live it." In the words of the Sammy Davis Jr. song popular about that time, "I Gotta Be Me." I went to bed that night not knowing how early I would have to get up to ride my bike that far. I didn't know how dark it would be, or what the best route was to take, but I was going to do it. Since I was so anxious, I hardly slept at all, so getting up early enough was not a problem. I hardly warmed the sheets before I was up again.

I set out about 5:30 a.m., and by the time I got to Forest Park, I realized that I was way ahead of schedule. I thought that on the last day of my life I should stop at the zoo and check out some of the animals one last time. Although I do think there will be animals in heaven, it would be a way to respect the planet one last time. At a particularly busy intersection in the financial district, a driver of a Cadillac lowered his window, shouted at me and made an obscene middle finger gesture indicating that he didn't think I deserved a place in the galaxy much less on the road. I felt sorry for his secretary and co-workers, realizing what an obnoxious grump he was before the day had even started. I arrived at Visitation Academy in my blue bike shorts and a burnt orange t-shirt. I picked orange because it's my favorite color and somewhat reflective. I didn't want to die in an accident before my last day was over. I arrived so early that only a thin trickle of students was coming in and there were only five cars on the parking lot. I rang the door at the convent and briefly explained my plan to the sister who answered. She was not impressed with my clerical outfit, but I was the best priest they had for the day. She showed me a guest room where I could rest. I didn't want to dirty the sheets so I laid down on the floor for a power nap. There was no shower or change of clothes in the plan, because this was the last day of my life, and I didn't have plans to waste water or smell good or be on the cover of GQ. After all, these girls were never going to see me again, so I just didn't give a darn.

I came down the center aisle of the gym when I was introduced as the priest leader of the day. I was pushing my red racing bike, wearing dark blue shorts and my orange t-shirt. I was self-conscious about my legs that earned me the nickname "bird legs" in college, but I didn't care, nobody there was going to see me again after today. With whatever else I may have said or however I embellished it, the main notion of my presentation was about how fear and trying to please others boxes us in while the freedom of living every day as if it were our last allows us to be who we really are. And who we are is this unique child of God, who envelopes and penetrates in every moment and situation of our lives. We also need to remember that God is omniscient, knows everything and forgets nothing, as God should be and hence appreciates and embraces every moment, every breath and blink, even while we are asleep. We can feel free, even exhilarated to be possessed by this good God. Carpe Diem!

Mev and her sister waited for me at the end of the day. She stood by her tan Chevy Nova making certain that I didn't need a ride home instead of riding my bike in the afternoon traffic. But who needed to pollute the environment with her driving me all the way back to the city when her home was just three miles away? It was the last day of my life, so I could take any risk that was called for to be faithful and live the day to the fullest. Besides, I needed to visit the zoo one more time. If the ride home didn't kill me, but just left me exhausted, I didn't have to worry about being too tired to get out of bed on the day after All Souls Day. On that day, the one after my last day, I would be one with all the souls in glory.

Months later, I was scheduled to help with another day of prayer at Visitation Academy. Mev didn't take part in the planning. I asked Sister and she said that Mev's family was on a trip. After several weeks went by, I called Mev's home to inquire about the trip. Her mom answered and told me that the family had gone to China. "Tell me what it was like to visit China," I inquired. "Well it's nothing like Africa," was the casual response.

"I don't think that helps me a lot. I was wondering whether it was anything like Cape Girardeau, Missouri." That brought a bit of a twitter, but it was clear that we were in two distinct universes. Later, I learned after talking to Mev that her family's travels always included out-of-the-way places and not just the local tourist traps. Her parents wanted the family to see what life was like where the poor and the working class lived. She had a world view that few could match. Their later travels would take her past the slums of Rio on the way to the Christ of the Andes statue and even to the city parks in Moscow, all of which was a far cry from a Carnival Cruise or from Cape Girardeau.

After graduating from St. Louis University, Mev got a position teaching theology at Visitation while she lived at the Catholic Worker House. She was a citizen of the world who could fit in and bring joy and energy to any setting and any group of people. One day she phoned me after school. "Father Gerry, I'm calling to see if you would be able to teach some of my classes at Visitation Academy."

"Well, I might be able to help," I replied somewhat tentatively. Really I had come to love Mev and like Visitation Academy so much that I was hiding my eager, "I-can-do it-let-me-at-it" response. "Would you like to tell me why you won't be teaching and why you think that I would be a good replacement?"

"I'll answer the second question first because it's easier," she replied with her typical perkiness. "I know that you will be a good replacement because I teach the girls out of the book you wrote, *The People Parish*. I think that you will be able to teach it without doing any class preparation since you wrote the book. Now how does that sound?"

"That's a pretty compelling reason," I conceded. "So now tell me why it is that you won't be teaching for the rest of this semester."

She started to explain something about ovarian cysts and surgery that she would have in the coming weeks. I always listen to what women tell me about their ailments and never pry into the details. It was shocking news, and I knew I would pray for her each time I drove to class and home again. Home now was St. Bridget Parish in the St. Louis housing projects.

I had overcome much of my fear and addressed my racism over the ten years since she had first come to Visitation East.

"I'll be happy to do it. Just send me a class schedule and a course outline, and I will try to do justice to the wonderful text that you are using." It was delightful hearing from her, but the news was not good. Fortunately I could not have predicted the future of the disease.

Later on, Mev went to Brazil to interview Archbishop Helder Camera as well as several unknown women who were working their way out of poverty. She also interviewed a cross section of church and political leaders. She wrote a book from these interviews entitled *The Struggle is One* and took pictures of all the folks she spoke with. She had a great talent for taking pictures and catching the eyes of subjects, especially children. Another time she made the international media was when she was the master of ceremonies for World Youth Day in Denver. Pope John Paul II was on camera for much of that day, and Mev was the commentator and a prophetic voice urging the Pope to consider the important role of women in the church. Those topics were part of a private conversation off camera.

I invited Mev to the celebration of my twenty-fifth anniversary as a priest in 1992. During that time, she was at the Jesuit School of Theology in Berkeley, California, studying for her doctorate. She sent me a note congratulating me and declining the invitation to come to St. Louis because of her studies and the deadline for her dissertation. Previous to that time she had published a book called *Faces of Poverty - Faces of Christ*. The book included photos she had taken around the world with essays on the facing pages written by her dear friend and mentor, Father John Kavanaugh, S.J., her favorite professor in her undergraduate years at Saint Louis University. On the flyleaf she wrote, "Dear Gerry, Thank you for teaching me many, many years ago how to live each day as if it were my last. Congratulations on your twenty-five years of service to the church. Love, Mev."

She had learned at the age of seventeen what many seventy-five-year-olds don't even consider. She knew how to live each day to the fullest. I was overjoyed, flattered, proud and humbled all at once. That book, and the stole my family gave me, are the only gifts that I remember from my twenty-fifth anniversary.

About that same time, St. Bridget's Parish was having a fund-raising auction. I thought that some of Mev's photos would be wonderful auction items. When I spoke with her, she agreed and was delighted to donate several. She said, "Call my parents and have them get some together out of the collection that I have at their house. Then you go and pick them up for the auction." I did that and the evening of the auction arrived. On the night of the auction, as I was looking over the bidding, I noticed that Mev's black and white photographs had not gotten the lofty bids I thought would have been appropriate. While I was tempted to outbid the competition, I reasoned that if I wanted some of Mev's work all I would have to do was to call Pete, Mev's dad, once again and ask for some. He would give them to me in a blink. But then I had second thoughts and decided to support the parish by raising the bids. I went home the proud possessor of four framed photos by Mev. It was one of those inspired decisions, because no one could have imagined what catastrophe would befall Mev in the next few months of her young life.

She had made the national news once more because she was selected by *U.S. Catholic* magazine as the layperson of the year. The award had hardly been bestowed when the shocking news about Mev saddened the entire social justice community of the church. Mev Puleo had been experiencing some vision problems, which were quickly diagnosed as inoperable brain tumors. I called Pete, "Yes, Father that's right. We hardly know what to do. If the news were that she could be treated any place in the world, we would fly her there on a charter flight. But nobody knows what to do." Firstly, I was crushed with the devastating news, but secondly I thought how inspired I was that night of the auction. I got the photos when they were available, because there isn't always time to call Mev and ask her for some more pictures. It was a very small matter, but it was a profound truth. Don't procrastinate, because there just isn't always more time. I learned: do what you have to do now, because it is the only time that you have. Don't live for the minute, live for the moment.

After this tragic news sunk in, I bolstered my courage and went to visit Pete and Evie at their home. Pete answered the door and welcomed me. As we shook hands I said, "Pete, you know that I have come here over the years to ask your financial support for one of my endeavors, but I trust that you always knew that I loved your family whether you helped me or not. You are very dear to me and I have been thinking about you and praying ever since I heard the news. So I came today to catch up on the latest and to pray with you."

Pete was a bit impetuous and welcomed me sincerely, but was quick to ask, "Father, did you see Mev on television with the Pope on World Youth Day?" Pete was as proud as any dad would be, but being Italian Catholic there was hardly a more important question than to ask someone about whether I had seen his daughter with the Pope. It didn't make any difference that the Pope was Polish.

"Pete, I'm embarrassed to say that I didn't see her, because it was on cable and I don't have cable television."

"Would you like to see it now? It was on all day, but I edited it all down to just the time that Mev and the Pope were on together. That is thirty-six minutes." It was an offer that I couldn't refuse, and that too sounded like a line from an Italian movie. "Sure, that would be a pleasure." But we had hardly gotten comfortable in front of the TV when the phone rang. It was Mev calling from California. There were enough extensions in the house that we were all able to chat and pray together. She would be coming home to St. Louis soon. Her health situation was becoming such that school was no longer a possibility.

While her family wanted Mev and her husband, Mark, to move to St. Louis and come to their comfortable, sprawling house for care, they made their own decision to live in a cozy century old brick home in a humbler city neighborhood and in a more vibrant parish community. They moved to St. Louis and bought a house in St. Cronan's Community where I am currently pastor. The church had a reputation for social justice and care of the least of our brothers and sisters. They bought a home on Arco and people in the parish community signed lists to prepare meals, take Mev to the doctor, and give her round-the-clock nursing care. She deteriorated quickly, and soon this famed photographer and eloquent television master of ceremonies for the papal visit was in a hospice program. With an eye for the camera that had an uncanny knack for catching the subject's lively eyes and a tongue eloquent enough for a television audience with the Pope on international TV, Mev could no longer see or speak.

On Tuesday mornings Mev and Mark had an early morning open house. They had a time of Buddhist prayer in their living room, and people were welcome to come to pray in silence after the monastery gong was rung three times to slowly invite people into prayerful silence. The day I went, Mev was stretched out on the couch and about eight people prayed in the candlelit space. Her luxurious, glossy black shoulder length hair that was her youthful Italian legacy when I first met her in high school had fallen victim to the cancer treatments. She had an inch of hair, having taken the last picture of herself while she could still see enough to set up the camera and pose. That picture would appear on her memorial card at her funeral. When I said goodbye to her after prayer that morning, she spoke one of the few four syllables that she could manage, "Bye."

Her father cried with me and tried to make sense out of the passing of such a precious servant who died so very young. I reminded him that she had written on the flyleaf of her book all that anyone needed to know to be prepared to leave this world. "Thank you for teaching me when I was very, very young how to live every day as if it were my last." At her funeral homily, her friend, Father Kavanaugh, reminded those who grieved her short, whirlwind life of her favorite prayer by Ignatius Loyola, "Take Lord, Receive." Mev, the missionary of compassion, the prolific photographer and energetic speaker had given her eyes to blindness and her tongue to muteness. However, she died with her vision of glory and her voice of praise and thanksgiving intact. Like Jesus, she was just thirty-three years old when she died.

When I was in my early teens, a thought took told of me: Jesus didn't die to save us from suffering—he died to teach us how to suffer .... Sometimes I actually mean it. I'd

*rather die young, having lived a life crammed with meaning,
than to die old, even in security, but without meaning.*

Mev Puleo from *All Saints* by Robert Ellsberg
(Crossroad, 1997)

FROM MEV'S HUSBAND, MARK CHMIEL

You did a great job in the chapter you sent,
capturing Mev's *joie de vivre* in the years long before I met
her. Such attention to the social context and concrete
detail make for engaging reading. You gave me some
vivid images of Mev at her Enneagram 3 best. Also,
you reminded me of a maxim I first learned of through
Maryknoll "First, Last, Only – live each day as if it were
your first, your last, and your only day on earth."

NATALIE WEST

"It is an act of faith to raise a child."

John Kavanaugh, S.J.

Jairus, a synagogue leader, came to Jesus, "My little daughter (twelve years old) is at the point of death. Come and lay your hands on her so that she may be made well and live." So he went with him.

MK 5:22-25

OVER THE 2011 THANKSGIVING HOLIDAYS, I received a call from Linda Boyer Johnson, a former employee from forty years ago. The call was a surprise, because she lives in Florida with her husband, and our communication was always cordial but intermittent. This was an emergency, because she was calling to tell me that her brother had died quite suddenly. I had known her deceased brother, Charles, through some family gatherings over the years. More recently, I had been his landlord as he rented an apartment from me. Through our landlord-tenant relationship, I became aware that he was quite a handyman and a jack-of-all trades. Whenever an elderly person in the neighborhood had a problem with a furnace or a light switch, some leaky plumbing, or a leaking roof, I would get Charles to survey the situation. He usually solved the problem quickly without a call to a costly authorized repair man. He had the tools and the talent to do the job, and everyone came away happy. Charles delighted in sharing his talents, although he appeared a bit smug to people who thought that the task was beyond him. Usually he was satisfied with whatever the person was able to pay, and he would be happy to wait for the money until the next Social Security check was at hand or even to the thirty-fifth of next month. He had a degree from a noted vocational school in St. Louis, but racism kept him out of the unions and therefore unemployed.

This background explains why I was at the Officer Funeral Home in East St. Louis, IL on the Friday after Thanksgiving in 2011. Since Charles had no church affiliation, I was asked to conduct a service for the family as a member of the family. Our relationship began when I hired his sister, Linda, as choir director at Visitation Church. Later, I celebrated her marriage to Dr. Gordon Johnson and subsequently I baptized two of their three sons. I would visit at their home and enjoy their gracious hospitality and even had a bedroom available if I chose to stay overnight. After their luscious wine dinners, it was better to stay put rather than tackle the interstate. Gordon called it Pater's Room.

Their son, Gareth, is a violin prodigy, and I attended several of his concerts when he performed with the St. Louis Symphony and at concerts in Florida. I also attended one of his recording sessions and was awed when his mother or his aunt Rene, Professor of Music Education at the College Conservatory of Music at the University of Cincinnati, would question the musicians about whether someone had missed a B flat eighth note in the 43rd measure of the piece. I would mull over the astonishing fact that all of these people had roots in East St. Louis, Illinois, a city more noted for poverty than for music. But knowledgeable people knew that other prodigies from there, Miles Davis and Clark Terry, recorded when there was no possibility of going back to correct an eighth note in the recording. In brief, I am saying that I am very much at home with this family and extremely blessed to be part of it.

As the folks were gathering to express their sympathy and celebrate the life of Charles, I found myself the only white person in this chapel with crystal chandeliers and a gun metal gray steel casket draped with the stars and stripes. Upholstered folding chairs stood in rows with couches lining the walls. About fifty African Americans filtered in dressed in stylish, subdued funeral attire with several women wearing hats appropriate for an Easter Sunday service in a Baptist Church. The family had several babies in arms, one obviously pregnant woman and an elder who shocked us all at the eulogy time by saying that she was ninety years young and a dear friend of Charles' mother, Ruth, who had gone to glory many years earlier.

As I was greeting people and introducing myself to some, an attractive young woman in a black business suit and heels approached me enthusiastically. She had a warm sparkle in her eyes as she spoke almost blurting out. "Father Gerry, I remember you when I was five years old. I told you that I went to St. Bernadette School, and you asked me if I knew who St. Bernadette was. When I said no, you sat me on your knee and told me the story of her life." It was a fuzzy and dim memory, but it was as real as yesterday to this vivacious woman who exuded the confidence of a Jeopardy contestant.

I couldn't place the face because two decades had gone by since this woman was five years old. Off hand, I didn't recall our earlier meeting, but once reminded, I began to remember the great story that Natalie held dear and shared so spontaneously. The pieces began to emerge. It had all the needed dramatic characters. The hero was a brave, wide-eyed, little girl, Bernadette; the place was obscure, Lourdes; her parents were worried and hurting; the crowd and police were menacing; and finally, the tortured parish priest felt caught between either a God moment apparition or a hoax. When Mary, the Mother of God, told Bernadette to stoop and scratch the hard earth, a spring bubbled up and transformed this backward place into a miraculous healing site. I hoped this story would be such a sacred connection to Natalie as to excite her with the notion of God speaking to her. It must have worked, because that's the story Natalie cherished. In Lourdes they built a big church and sick people who washed in the spring are healed to this day.

That's the story I told Natalie, a curious little girl who was all ears. She went to a school named for a little girl who was all ears to God talk through Mary the Mother of Jesus. I'm sure when I asked her about her school named for Bernadette, I would have asked a similar question if she attended a school named for Neil Armstrong. I would have told her about the moon landing and "One small step for man; one giant step for mankind."

"I'm Natalie, Linda's niece and Margaret's daughter," she responded. She was smiling and spoke with self-confidence, even polish. She continued without flourish, "I graduated from Washington University in 2007 and now I work in the Alumni Development Office."

The fact that she had remembered me after so many years and had spoken to me in this room full of people certainly enhanced my confidence. I stood there returning her joyous smile while doing some quick math. I figured that she graduated at the age of 21 so she must be 26 or 27 years old now. I was humbled that she remembered me so clearly after twenty-one years. I inquired further about her background and preparation that landed her a job in a major university's development office.

"Oh, I studied Women and Gender Studies. I figured that gave me a broad background and the ability to think critically. I can do whatever I'd like to do. Now I am studying for a graduate degree in International Affairs."

"What would you like to see come out of those studies?"

"I'm not sure, but I knew that I ought to continue my education while I am working at Washington U. because I can get 50% off on my tuition. I can't pass that up!" she exclaimed. "When I'm done, I would like to see the world and be a travel writer"

I told her that I had written a couple of books. "Now I'm working on a new one that many people question whether a priest knows anything about. I am writing a book about my wonderful relationships with children. How's that sound to you in today's world?"

"Oh, I should be included in your book," she announced boastfully and without batting an eye. In fact, she was standing a bit more at attention. We had just heard several people comment about Charles as the consummate soldier so this was a good pose for Natalie to assume.

I didn't need any convincing that she ought to be included in my book. I was still breathless about the fact that my storytelling had been so memorable to a five-year-old. I wanted to ask her what she remembered of my story, but I didn't want to put her on the spot. However, graduates of Washington University are among the brighter stars in the academic galaxy, so I'm confident that my question would have elicited more than a blank stare. However, I gave her my card and invited her to come and worship in our church. I made an offhand promise that inclusion in my book was a given. She looked at the church address and stated that her apartment was six blocks away. This was the second happy accident of the day.

I hope to see more of her without waiting another two decades. As far as I'm concerned as a writer, pastor and family friend, she should be included in my life and in my book. I can hardly wait for the book of her travels. I'm sure her life will have many chapters I wouldn't want to miss.

FROM NATALIE WEST

> Father Gerry, I hope you are well! Please see the attached corrections. It was a great read. I am so sorry it took me so long. I have been swamped at work. I had three events yesterday welcoming 1,650 freshmen and their families to campus. I am just glad I am finished with that. I won't have any big events now until October and November. Tomorrow I am off to New York to leave for China.
>
> Talk to you soon, Natalie

University of Notre Dame –
Moreau Seminary

LIFE UNDER THE GOLD DOME at the University of Our Lady in South Bend, Indiana was both exhilarating and intimidating. There was the Fighting Irish pride and spirit and the intellectual energy and curiosity of bright students eager to be challenged. Faculty members had double doctorates while I had a B.A. from a small catholic seminary. Champagne-bubbly co-eds jogged around the lakes while I had an uninformed celibate's fear of women and a terror of bright and beautiful ones.

I learned much at Notre Dame, hardly anything trackable by grades. Most of all I learned about Gerry Kleba. I came as a pastoral theology teacher and formation director at Moreau Seminary. I stuck my toe into other areas of campus life especially at the Center for Social Concerns, and I departed there a better student of life.

GERALD J. KLEBA

"BE SHEPHERDS LIVING WITH THE SMELL OF THE SHEEP"

Pope Francis said, "Some people continue to defend trickle-down theories which assume that economic growth...will inevitably succeed in bringing about greater justice and inclusiveness in the world. This opinion, which has never been confirmed by the facts, expresses a crude and naïve trust in the goodness of those wielding economic power and in the sacralized workings of the prevailing economic system. Meanwhile, the excluded are still waiting. To sustain a lifestyle which excludes others, or to sustain enthusiasm for that selfish ideal, a globalization of indifference has developed. Almost without being aware of it, we end up being incapable of feeling compassion at the outcry of the poor, weeping for other people's pain, and feeling a need to help them. The culture of prosperity deadens us." Ibid. *Evangelii Gaudium*. P, 47.

In the *Saint Louis Review* Elizabeth Wimmer wrote:
"While most Notre Dame students were still busy celebrating their football team's Fiesta Bowl victory and number-one ranking, some students chose to spend a portion of their Christmas vacation in the inner city.

Seventeen students from Notre Dame and St. Mary's College of South Bend, IN, participated in Notre Dames's "Urban Plunge" in St. Louis — the largest number of students ever here for the program, according to Father Gerald J. Kleba, the coordinator of the program here.

"For kids to want to do something like that, it's heroism," Father Kleba said. "Urban Plunge has caused some people to change their major and their whole lives."

Theresa Kelly, a junior from Rochester, IL, said the group had discussed why they had chosen to go on an Urban Plunge. "A lot of us said that we live sheltered lives and had things handed to us on a silver platter."

she said. Also, "Notre Dame is extremely upper-middle class" and some students wanted to experience life in the inner city, she said.

Most of the students said they had never spent any time in the inner city before, and some said they had been concerned that they would be unwelcome because people would classify them as "rich people." However, the group said they found that the people they met were friendly and welcoming and that the inner city was not as scary as they thought, at least with a guide who knew the area and people."

January 27, 1989. p. 9.

ERICA DAHL-BREDINE

'Prophets of a future not our own'

It helps, now and then, to step back and take the long view. The Kingdom is not only beyond our efforts, it is even beyond our vision. We accomplish in our lifetime only a tiny fraction of the magnificent enterprise that is God's work.

Nothing we do is complete, which is another way of saying that the Kingdom of God lies beyond us. No statement says all that should be said. No prayer fully expresses our faith. No confession brings perfection, no pastoral visit brings wholeness. No program accomplishes the Church's mission. No set of goals and objectives includes everything. This is what we are about. We plant the seeds that one day will grow. We water seeds already planted, knowing that they hold future promise. We lay foundations that will need further development. We provide yeast that produces effects far beyond our capabilities. We cannot do everything, and there is a sense of liberation in realizing that this enables us to do something, and to do it very well.

It may be incomplete but it is a beginning, a step along the way, an opportunity for the Lord's grace to enter and do the rest. We may never see the end results, but that is the difference between the master builder and the worker. We are workers, not master builders, ministers, not messiahs. We are prophets of a future that is not our own. Amen.

"Prayer of a Prophet," Archbishop Oscar Romero

"WHAT COMES TO MIND when you hear Notre Dame, Winston Churchill, and Archbishop Oscar Romero?" If that were my question in a word association game, the answer would be Erica Dahl-Bredine. My admission to the University of Notre Dame in South Bend, Indiana as a pastor in residence without a graduate degree was one of the more awesome and intimidating experiences of my life.

I would teach some classes at this legendary institution all the while wondering whether I would have been able to pass the student entrance exam. While other people there boasted double doctorates from iconic universities, I had a B.A. in Philosophy from Cardinal Glennon College, a seminary in St. Louis. My assigned task at Notre Dame was to help prepare seminarians for the priesthood. I lived at the all male Moreau Seminary separated from the Gold Dome and the gothic spire of Sacred Heart Basilica on campus by St. Joseph Lake.

On the opposite side of the lake, one of the places that drew me like a magnet was the two-story brick box structure that housed the Center for Social Concerns. It was the brain child of a Holy Cross Father named Don McNeill whose dad had charged up the airwaves of NBC radio in the early days with a daily broadcast from the Hotel Sherman in Chicago. It was called "Don McNeill's Breakfast Club." Young Don had starred on Notre Dame's basketball team and then entered the seminary to join the priests at his Alma Mater.

It took the University of Our Lady a long time to welcome women students, but by the time that I came there in 1983, they were very well established and sometimes outnumbered the men in the freshman class. Needless to say, the seminary that I attended did not embrace women students and the seminarians at Notre Dame were much healthier and more open and much less cocooned. In fact, our primitive teaching about the call to priestly celibacy cautioned us about the wiles of women and warned us to "beware of female girls of the opposite sex." They were the enemy. It was not likely to inspire us to the full humanity of the gospels. Jesus said, "I come that you may have life and have it more abundantly." Rather than abundance, the seminary prepared us for a portion of life so small that if listed on a menu it would have been under Kids' Plates.

Hence, I was stunted in social and emotional development. The large numbers of brilliant and beautiful women on the campus made my head spin and wonder about my commitment to celibacy. One of these co-eds was a particularly spunky, sparkling, and smart freshman named Erica.

I encountered her on several occasions at the Center for Social Concerns, a place that became my second home.

The heart of my previous fifteen years of pastoral ministry was formed by a document from the First Synod of Catholic Bishops after Vatican II that proclaimed, "Action on behalf of social justice is a constitutive element of gospel living." I tried to embody that goal of social action in several ways in my parish assignments in St. Louis. At those parishes, I worked with people to start a credit union, a Montessori pre-school, a housing corporation, and the building of nursing homes. I even worked to care for Mother Earth getting a sanitary landfill in Ste. Genevieve to replace the city dump that collected trash on the banks of the Mississippi – only to have the spring flood clean it out and send the contents to the Gulf of Mexico.

After encountering Erica during several programs and service projects at the C.S.C., I invited her to join me for a Coke. We sat down and I began. "Erica, you intrigue me and dazzle me with some of the things that you have to say. You are certainly a bright and energetic young woman. I would like to know a bit more about your life. Please tell me something about yourself, where you're from and what makes you tick."

I couldn't have been more surprised when she began to respond with an ease and openness that I soon learned was typical of her. "First I have to tell you something curious about you asking me these questions. In brief, I'm from New Mexico, but my mother came from Missouri and my grandfather was the dean of Westminster College in Fulton, Missouri. My mother was five years old when Winston Churchill visited the college for the talk that became known as Churchill's 'Iron Curtain' speech. She used to talk about her vivid memory of seeing him and President Truman when they arrived."

"My mom and dad met each other when they were students at Carleton College in Northfield, Minnesota. Although neither of them had any experience with Catholicism, they were both very interested in the Catholic faith and had many conversations about it. They got married right after college and spent the next year in Spain and then another year in Saskatchewan, Canada teaching in a small country high school. There they had some powerful experiences of Catholicism that led them to begin a more formal inquiry process. They finally entered the Church in grad school at Northwestern University. It was there that my mom discovered a copy of the Catholic Worker paper one day with a woodcut of St. Francis and His Lady Poverty on the front. She was so taken with it that she grabbed it up and ran home to my Dad, waving it and practically shouting, "WHAT IS THIS?" They read it all and knew suddenly that was why they had become Catholics. So at the next spring break, they bundled me up, I was 3 months at the time, and took off for New York to meet Dorothy Day, one of the founders of the Catholic Worker House. They then moved into a Catholic Worker-Franciscan community in inner-city Chicago known as The Gospel Family. The neighborhood around the house wasn't safe, or a good place for kids to play outside. So after their third child was born, they moved to a farm at a Franciscan Friary in Wisconsin, 70 miles north of Chicago, to build a rural extension of the Catholic Worker community."

"During our time there, three more children were born. We then moved to Silver City, New Mexico in the Las Cruces, New Mexico diocese. My dad was asked by the Bishop to serve as parish administrator, because there was no priest available. My mother founded a bilingual Montessori preschool. My parents also began working across the border in Mexico in several community projects. We built our own family home out of adobe bricks that we all made together, while living in a very small rented house in town. Once I got into Notre Dame, I became so spoiled with having my own room here that I vowed that I will never make another adobe in my life."

Wow! In less time than it took us to drink one Coke I had heard the outline of the adventurous life story of a family that had produced this warm, joyful and exuberant, no nonsense young lady. Impressive indeed, and so was her glowing smile and her calm serenity that reminded me of a Buddhist monk who was instructing the new novices. Erica was a walking manifestation of the church's social doctrine that was enshrined on posters on the walls of the Center for Social Concerns. Bumper stickers were available, "If you want peace, work for justice," (Pope Paul VI).

"Oh," I said, "there is one more thing that I am curious about. Tell me about your hyphenated last name."

"My mother's name is Kathy Dahl and my father's name is Phil Bredine," she responded with a casual teasing grin. "And that's where I got the name Dahl-Bredine." I knew that I should have guessed it, but that is only in hindsight. I had never met anyone who explained their last name in that fashion before. Now thirty years later, it is much more commonplace especially in my own parish family.

We went on some retreats together, and she came to a talk that I gave on Spirituality and Social Justice. I would have her over for dinner at Moreau Seminary occasionally, and I would listen as she got into some challenging conversations with the seminarians, especially those who had spent some time before seminary in the Jesuit Volunteers or the Holy Cross Associates. I invited her to talk about her life and vision to the seminarians. While they were four to six years her senior, she surpassed many of them in her maturity and understanding of gospel values.

When her parents came to visit, I was eager to meet them. After that visit, it became even easier for me to understand her life and her passion for justice and equality. Kathy told me, "As parents, we want to raise our kids to have strong wings and deep roots, to know where their home is and that the world is their home."

Our shared interest in the social gospel was continually reinforced by our participation in programs and activities at the C.S.C. These revolved around student outreach to poor areas of South Bend. We shared simple meals at the center to build community and awareness of international concerns. This was done through Pax Christi and the participation of Holy Cross Associates who had served in a developing country. These activities were balanced with regular retreat opportunities.

At no time did the big issues of war, peace and violence come closer to the U.N.D. campus than in the spring of 1985. As graduation approached, there was always speculation about who would be the commencement speaker. The selection of that person, who would also receive an honorary doctorate, was always the personal decision of the legendary president of the university, Father Theodore Hesburgh. It was questionable if he consulted anyone regarding this decision, but it is certain that he did not take nominations from the graduates. In 1985, Father Ted, as he liked to be called, announced that the speaker would be the first graduate of the university to become the national leader of a country. Additionally, that person was a man whom Father Ted had taught during his years as an undergraduate. The person was none other than the president of El Salvador, Napoleon Duarte. Since Father Ted knew him since his youth, he referred to this international leader as Nappy.

This news caused more than a few raised eyebrows and ripples of concern. There was a questioning, negative reaction in the daily student newspaper, but there was an even noisier outcry among the rank and file of the C.S.C. "How could the University of Our Lady honor someone who was heading up the death squad government of the country named for Our Savior?" This was the regime that had killed and kidnapped tens of thousands and now their leader would be put in the brightest spotlight available at U.N.D. It was beyond comprehension. The question was asked, "If Archbishop Romero had been a Holy Cross bishop, and if the four U.S. religious women who were raped and murdered had been Holy Cross Sisters and Associates, would the university have invited President Duarte?" Many on campus rolled their eyes and asked the hard questions, but if these ever got Hesburgh's attention; they had no impact in terms of reversing the decision and disinviting Duarte. One wondered, "How could such a major blunder have occurred?"

These were the questions and issues that swirled around the Center for Social Concerns. However, at the administrative center of the university, the visit of internationally famous alum was a grand accomplishment to be proudly paraded before the grads and their families. When there was no doubt that the show would go on, dissidents at the C.S.C. met to plan an appropriate response to this appalling embarrassment. To those active at the center, it was adjudged to be a bold-faced, headline statement supporting war, torture, rape, trauma and every other type of abuse all personified in President Duarte. This could not go forward in silence. Late night meetings in prayerful settings finally led people to adopt a two-pronged response on behalf of social justice. One was to blight the celebratory mood of graduation week with street theatre interruptions that portrayed the kidnapping, arrests and beatings of innocent bystanders in the same fashion as these atrocities that occurred in the villages and on the street corners throughout El Salvador. The second decision was one that involved me and called for as much courage as I could possibly muster. People would make huge banners with the names of Oscar Romero, S. Ita Ford, lay volunteer Jean Donovan, S. Dorothy Kazel and S. Maura Clarke. These would be brought to the graduation ceremony during the commencement address by President Duarte. They would be displayed in silent, public protest before the 17,000 people gathered at the Athletic and Convocation Center to celebrate graduation.

The strategists at the C.S.C. were looking for five gutsy people who would dare to create a banner and make a scene on that day. After torturous mental deliberation, after I told myself a thousand reasons why I should not do this, I finally signed up to be Oscar Romero for the demonstrations at the graduation in May 1985. I was miserable every minute after raising my hand and volunteering at the meeting. If I had ever stepped out of my comfort zone it was that May at Notre Dame. All I could tell myself was that Archbishop Romero, who was the former confidant of the rich and powerful, had a total transformation and became fully present to the poor and the no-accounts. If he could be that Christ-like and be murdered at the altar during Mass, I could risk standing up and wearing his mantle for a moment. I knew I should risk being shunned at a social event as preparation for some prophetic moment I might be called to in later life.

It was decided that the five of us who were to be banner carriers would really be bed sheet carriers. We gathered at the center to paint late at night. Using a white bed sheet, and blue paint we painted the name of our hero on it in bold block letters that would be visible throughout the stadium. I decided to paint mine in royal blue to match my blue eyes.

Since I am six foot four inches, I have a wide wingspan and could hold the banner boldly. We gathered at the center to paint late at night and soon the mid-May graduation was upon us. During graduation week, the street theatre violence and masked kidnappings went on several dozen times in main quadrangles and wooded, lonely trails on campus. It was disruptive and frightening. It marred the usual party atmosphere surrounding commencement at Notre Dame. Many parents who had paid mega-bucks for an outstanding Catholic education were questioning and angry. They were downright disgusted that this beautiful graduation rite of spring could not have been flawless, undisturbed, serene, and even elegant. A prevailing notion was, "This isn't the time or place for such disruptive shenanigans under the guise of raising questions of conscience. It undermined the solemnity of this special moment. These things are for another time and place or maybe should be saved for a classroom discussion next year when classes resume."

To these people, it was an intrusive, uncalled-for act by hippies who were twenty years too late. In the Vietnam era, Father Ted had forbidden protests on campus. Why couldn't he have taken as firm a stance with these boisterous rabble-rousers? Maybe things had changed in twenty years even at tradition-bound Notre Dame. Everyone knew that the week was to celebrate graduates, God, country, and Notre Dame. If some people don't like it, they can just leave and go to school somewhere else.

Graduation day arrived, and President Duarte of El Salvador arrived on campus also. The Secret Service arrived, too, and everyone who entered the commencement area needed a ticket and had to pass a security checkpoint. These were the days before 9/11, even before metal detectors. However, it was a time when bags and parcels were inspected. In our planning for the event, we determined that the banners would be brought into the hall by wrapping them tightly around our bodies from the armpits down to the waist. I dressed in my black suit and Roman collar and shiny Florsheims and set out for the graduation looking as clerical and proper as possible. If my clothes were neat, my guts were rumpled, and my brain was in a tizzy. I was assigned to select a seat on the bleachers in the upper deck close to the railing where I would be highly visible. I went early to get my desired seat. I could appreciate Jonah on his way to Nineveh choosing to go the opposite direction and getting swallowed by that big fish. I too wanted to go the other direction. I wanted to get on my bike and go to the Indiana Dunes and lay in the sun by Lake Michigan. However, I went to graduation.

I found an open seat next to a family from Cleveland. The grandparents of the graduate had never been to Notre Dame before and could not have been prouder. While they had some family members who had graduated from college, all of them had gone to some no-name school that was little better than a diploma mill. Finally, they had a grandson graduating from Notre Dame. They knew that Harvard and Oxford were dwarfed by the stature of Notre Dame, because Notre Dame was Catholic. When they saw a priest coming to take the empty place on the bench near them, they could not have been more welcoming. They were flattered to have me as company, but wondered aloud why I would not be seated someplace more prominent as would befit the dignity of a priest. When they found out that I was on the staff of the seminary, they were even more gracious. "Why are you sitting way up here? Certainly, you could have gotten a better seat. We are lucky to be here, but if we could have gotten better seats than these we sure would have taken them."

I made some offhand comment that I had been seated on stage with the priests before at last year's graduation, so I thought that I would try this expansive view this year. Besides I'm not a Holy Cross priest, but a priest on loan from St. Louis. I'm the director of the diocesan seminarians. That satisfied them because they weren't much interested in my trivia. They were quite eager to tell me more about their pride and joy graduate and his accomplishments and dreams. However, they were impressed that I taught my students one course in prayer and another in spirituality and social justice. I'm sure they thought I was the person who led the evening rosary at Our Lady's Grotto. All in all, it was a friendly exchange that was saturated with exuberance both at the richness of this family event and the added distinction of sharing this space with a priest who taught at this glittering home of Fighting Irish football. As the strains of *Pomp and Circumstance* accompanied the faculty entrance, excitement was palpable and my audible stomach growling almost had me heading for the men's room. While I pretended to relish the warmth and conversation with the Clevelanders, in truth I was totally distracted and mentally reviewing our agreed upon rules of our demonstration.

1. Don't display your banner until the introduction of President Duarte.
2. Only stand and hold up your banner during applause time, so that no one can complain that you are blocking their view.
3. If one of you gets arrested or escorted out of the hall, the others will continue with the demonstration.

All of those commitments were clear and doable. There were just a few questions I had for myself. Do I have the courage to even open my shirt, loosen my belt and tug away to pull out the tightly wrapped banner? If I do have the courage to stand at the ovations, will any of the others be standing too, or will I be the only one? If people around me boo and shout, will I be calm and persist with the demonstration or will I rush for the nearest exit? As I thought about all these things, I prayed for courage, I prayed for the four others, and I prayed even more fervently that the electricity would fail, the lights would go out and the ceremony cancelled as a divine sign of God's rage. Finally, it was time for Father Ted to introduce his freshman theology student, President Nappy.

As he began the introduction, I took off my coat and laid it across my lap. Then I started to unbutton my shirt and pull it out of my pants. My neighbors from Cleveland, who had become wedged on our crowded bleacher bench, began to move further away from me. Their faces looked scared and angry. They were probably recalling some recent street theatre of masked military dragging some kicking young women into a van with Tommy guns drawn. Their faces suggested their outrage and fear regarding my possible next move. If the white sheet I was pulling out had been a Burmese Python, they could not have been more distant and petrified. With the space I had been given, I now had room to unfold my banner and make sure that the letters were right side up. As I did the actions that I had carefully choreographed in my bedroom, my bladder kept telling me that I had to go to the bathroom, right now. I tried to ignore the urgency of that call which was something I had never rehearsed. The intro was concluded, the applause was thunderous and without much thinking I stood bolt upright and threw open my arms proclaiming, OSCAR ROMERO. I made a bit of a pirouette so as to give more people the opportunity to view my handiwork and read my proclamation. As the applause died down, I seated myself. The space left for me could have held three people. These people knew I was contagious and none of them wanted anything to do with that priest whose original popularity had plummeted to disdain. As I was seating myself and gathering my banner, I sighed in relief noticing some of the other banners that had caught my attention. The others had stood up, and I was proud to be with them rather than staying seated and letting them down. There were a dozen applause lines and each time I stood I found it easier, and the tension subsided.

After the talk, I sat there folding my banner because my role in the protest was complete. I tried to compress it so small that I could carry it out under my arm. None of the Cleveland visitors returned to any seat close to me, so I had room to stretch out. I was present to Archbishop Oscar Romero, but I was a pariah to all of my former neighbors. Only an hour earlier, I was a cherished priestly presence, but now I was a prophet who was not acceptable on my own campus among my own people. They were applauding an alumnus who headed a military regime. I was protesting a graduation that had been downgraded into a blessing of brutality.

Later on in the evening, we protesters gathered at the C.S.C. to debrief and evaluate our activities during graduation week. There was a sense of pride and relief with the faithful completion of the endeavor, but no great sense of accomplishment. There was general consensus that we had accomplished little more than consciousness raising by being determined enough to stand up for the poor and downtrodden. Had we changed anyone? We would never know for certain, but we did know that we had not been changed and had not sacrificed our core values. We also knew that we could stand up in the face of an unsympathetic crowd. A former parishioner, who was a Mark Twain type character, would often say, "Those who don't stand for something will fall for anything." Many of the disappeared of El Salvador would never be discovered, but we had stood up for them and not disappeared under the slight pressure we faced. We all agreed that was to our credit.

With my two-year teaching stint at Notre Dame now over, I returned to parish work in St. Louis. As I drove away, the banner that I had raised at graduation was suspended from my window sill overlooking the campus, 'blowin' in the wind.' Bob Dylan said that the answers to these complex issues were not simple but fragile and complex. "The answer, my friend, is blowin' in the wind; the answer is blowin' in the wind."

Erica graduated and went to work in war torn El Salvador. She was a volunteer at the parish orphanage of Mary, Mother of the Poor. I went to El Salvador as part of a peace and understanding program to support the peasants who were facing the repressions of a death squad government in 1989. It had been ten years since the four sisters from the U.S. had been kidnapped, raped and murdered. Archbishop Oscar Romero had been shot celebrating Mass with the sisters in the chapel of a Catholic hospital. When I accepted the invitation to go with the St. Louis contingent of the Latin American Solidarity Group, I couldn't say whether I was more interested in visiting with Erica or in following the travel itinerary for the group. Everyone in the group understood my wishes when I told them of my relationship with Erica and her commitment to the poor. While I only introduced her to the whole group in a brief moment together, it was safe to say that she was the embodiment of what all of us were about during our brief stay. We all had an airline ticket to return home in fourteen days; Erica was staying there for three years.

During my time with Erica at Mary, Mother of the Poor, we walked down railroad tracks where slum dwellers raised their children ten feet from the right of way. We climbed steep paths to shacks barely clinging to the hillsides and where my height prevented me from standing upright in their dwellings. It seemed like the houses were perched there and must have been deeply rooted like trees, because a simple foundation would never have held. We went to poor churches where people prayed, sang jubilantly and lit candles. We went to the tomb of Archbishop Romero in an unfinished cathedral where his sarcophagus area was plastered with signs and notes attesting to miracles worked through his intercession. Other notes were prayers of petition for future miracles. The cathedral remained half finished because the wealthy saw Romero as a pathetic communist prelate, and they refused to donate for the completion of the edifice. At the same time, the poor swarmed over the holy site with awe and quiet reverence.

But the highlight was seeing the children in the orphanage. I wondered if there might be an uprising if the bishop in a wealthy U.S. diocese decided to dedicate a parish to Mary, Mother of the Poor. The children were all smiles when Erica brought me into one of the classrooms where the children were working on an art project. There were brightly colored, lively murals on all the walls of the building. It stood in stark contrast to the ramshackle world outside the compound. All of the more secure buildings had walls around them with broken glass shards imbedded in the concrete top of the wall to ward off intruders. These may have been protection from vandals, but they could not deter the dreaded death squads. Erica told them that I was her friend from the U.S. The children were little of course, but some of their guardians and caregivers asked why people in the U.S. hate them so much and send money to kill them. I was red-faced and silent. The place was aglow, the faces alive, but the questions were stark. The welcome was frenzied, because of their love for Erica; but the suspicions were real. The woman who ran the orphanage said, "For a couple in El Salvador to replace themselves in the census count, they need to have eight children. Two of them will die in childbirth or infancy, two of them will be killed by the death squads, two of them will immigrate to another country. That leaves two to stay in El Salvador to replace their

parents." It was a dismal perspective, but it helped to broaden my definition of "pro-life."

I was reunited with the St. Louis group on the day we were to visit
a peasant village called Guarjila. Over the years, the people of this rural community had been driven out by the death squads and many fled
to refugee camps in Nicaragua. This town had been adopted by several
churches from St. Louis and through thick and thin received support in
the form of medicine, household items, and money. Now some villagers
had returned to repopulate the village. A highlight of our visit was to see
them, receive their thanks, and support them by our presence into the
questionable, but certainly unstable, future.

On the day of our Guarjila excursion, we boarded the white vans
we had rented and left our hotel in downtown San Salvador. Street
corners were still piled high with wreckage, debris, concrete and rebar from
buildings that had been destroyed by an earthquake ten years earlier. All
day, every day helicopters flew over with open doors and soldiers perched
in view with machine guns ready. I had never been in such a threatening war zone setting and the pavement shook underfoot as the helicopter
rotors clattered with teeth chattering rhythm.

Soon, we were out of the city and into the tropical lushness that
is the El Salvador countryside. It was October; the air was fresh and
the wildflowers luxuriant. However, the road was less congenial than the
natural surroundings. The cracks and potholes gave us assurance that
originally this had been a paved road, and progress was jarringly slow.

After two hours, as we arrived in Guarjila, only to be stopped at a
military roadblock. The uniformed, heavily-armed soldiers made us get
out of the van. Our bilingual members and drivers stepped forward to
talk with the soldiers. I had learned early, ever since my kindergarten class
photo, "tall boys in the back." My height made me more obvious, and my
slight Spanish was of no use in this situation. My ability to read body language and facial cues assured me that this was not a welcome party and this
tall boy wanted to follow the kindergarten rule so badly to be back home in

St. Louis. We were ordered to get back into the vans. We then followed an army truck that led us to a military base in the middle of nowhere.

As we drove along in the van, feeling like we were on the Trail of Tears, we reviewed the behavior that we had committed ourselves to follow when we were planning the trip. When we arrived at the outpost, we were ordered to line up at the counter, present our identification, and state the purpose for our visit to El Salvador. They demanded to know why we were in that part of the country. To my great chagrin, the man at the counter took our passports and put them into a locked drawer. Without my passport, I felt as naked and vulnerable as I would have felt without my clothes. The men and women in the group were sent to separate areas to sit and relax. It would be more accurate to say: sit and brood, sit and seethe, sit and pray. I sat on an outside porch looking beyond the military compound at the green hillside. Since I had represented Oscar Romero at the U.N.D. graduation, it wasn't hard to recall his fate or the tragedy of the U.S. women religious. Several hours went by that felt like an eternity, and I wondered how many people who are innocent actually spend years on death row. Was I sitting on death row and not even knowing it?

Finally, we were summoned back to the room where our passports were kept and an official took us to the office of the commandant. There we were seated randomly in a casual large office with military photos, decorations, and a flag planted near the officer's desk. The commandant welcomed us to El Salvador in perfect English. He asked several of us to say a little about ourselves and our occupations. I had put down "teacher" on a paper I filled out to come to the country thinking this might be a better identifier than "priest." Since we had already visited the heavily guarded, armed and blockaded U.S. Embassy, we knew that he had been informed of our presence. He saw us as clueless, well-intentioned, but naive simpletons, a Forest Gump community of rubes, who underestimated what a great service the U.S. government was providing the world by supporting the El Salvadoran military. The U.S. sponsored their "elite anti-terrorist" to come to the School of the Americas in Fort Benning, GA to learn the latest in torture, interrogation, and killing techniques.

He told us, "I don't want to say that you fine people are naïve, but you have to appreciate what an important job your neighbors here are doing to stop communism in Central America before you find that it is on your doorstep in Arkansas." When he said Arkansas, I was shocked to think that he knew U.S. geography or that the script prepared for him by the U.S. Embassy staff was so site specific. He continued, "The people in Guarjila whom you want to visit are the same sympathizers who hide the communist guerrillas and make it so difficult for us to enjoy the same peace in El Salvador that you have in the U.S." The lecture continued for thirty minutes in this same vein, until he felt we were all appropriately reprimanded and belittled. Throughout it, I wondered if they had a jail large enough to hold us, if they had a killing field, and if our passports had already been burnt.

Finally, when our shock therapy session was over he told us, "You can leave now. You must not continue, but return to San Salvador. Your passports are at the counter where you came in." He pushed his barrel-chested, medal-laden self up from the high-backed, leather executive chair behind the mahogany desk and came to shake hands with each of us as a junior officer led us back to be reunited with our passports. His vice-grip hand reminded me who was in charge. I remembered Paul's line to the Philippians, "Your citizenship is in heaven." I believe that and longed for that to the full, but not on this particular moment of this October afternoon. We returned to our downtown hotel. We later visited with people from Guarjila who walked through the countryside to San Salvador to greet us and bring us gifts. They were touched by the risks we took in facing the Army and sacrificing our passports, the same risks they face everyday.

A few nights later, we visited the University of Central America, UCA, a Jesuit university that the government considered the think tank of operatives behind the guerrilla movement. The priests saw themselves as followers of martyred Archbishop Romero siding with the peasants. His picture was on the college chapel wall along side their founder, St. Ignatius Loyola. We spent several hours visiting with two of the faculty members who spoke English; one taught theology and the other architecture. They described the situation of terror and oppression of the masses by the government under the direction of the mega-rich oligarchy known as the fourteen families of El Salvador. The architecture teacher told us how he was dedicated to designing adequate housing for the poor who had become homeless through the ruthless destruction of villages like Guarjila. The theology teacher taught a call to justice and rejection of torture, repression, and violence. They both threatened the system in making their fundamental option for the poor, but they confidently assured us that while they were harassed, they would never be arrested or killed. "We would be the front page story in the New York Times and the lead story on the NBC Nightly News. Neither the El Salvadoran government nor the U.S. State Department want that to happen. We know that in the eyes of God we are no more important than the poorest of the poor who are casually disappeared everyday and lie in shallow unmarked graves. But in the eyes of the world, we priests with degrees from the world's finest universities would be noticed, and so our deaths would be held up to public scrutiny." They were sure that they were safe as they spoke, but having just been detained and subject to indoctrination, I wasn't so sure. They certainly had more faith than I did. Sadly, they were both executed, shot in the head, three weeks later on November 16, 1989. I was right, and they were right. They made headlines around the world, and the world was outraged.

Erica's stay in El Salvador was a prelude to further studies. After her time in El Salvador she went to the University of Texas in Austin to study Latin American Issues. She went to El Salvador first so that she could speak Spanish well and have firsthand experience understanding the area. With that preparation, she would not be duped by some political double-talk spewed by academics that lived in their heads, but never knew the life faced by the people in the barrios. When she graduated, she got a job with Catholic Relief Services to work with indigenous people in the northeast part of Brazil. In Brazil, she had to stumble along with her Spanish until she became fluent in Portuguese."

After her time in Brazil and then Peru, Erica resigned from Catholic Relief Services because she wanted to come back to the U.S. She also wanted eventually to get married and have children before her biological clock stopped ticking. She moved back to Silver City for a time, but her parents left to become Maryknoll Lay Missioners in southern Mexico. While Erica was catching her breath, CRS told her that they wanted her to work in the U.S. They needed someone to oversee what was going on at the border given that the American immigration policy was in such disarray. I visited her in Tuscon and stayed with her in her small adobe home in an old neighborhood. The adobe home was quaint and charming, but I didn't have to make any of the bricks or lay them out in the sun as Erica had in her pre-Notre Dame years. The twenty years that had passed since I had first met this perky freshman had treated Erica much better than me. I was gray haired, soft and sixty. She had matured, her golden hair was sandier and her confident smile radiated joy. She was exuberant about life and still lit up the sky on a glaringly bright Arizona day.

She drove me to a border crossing in the town of Douglas, Arizona where we parked and walked past the border guards into Mexico. I never imagined that we could cross so freely for about 25 miles into the country with no questions asked. I knew there would be questions when we wanted to cross back to the U.S., so I had my passport handy. We visited the jail to see some of the people who had been captured by the border guards and were waiting to be sent back home. It was a hard setting with concrete bunks and nothing to do for hours but talk to a few cellmates. These people would stay until there were enough going to their part of the country to fill a bus and go back home. Some were clear in their goal. "I will just try to cross again." A roundly pregnant woman in her twenties tried to get comfortable on the hard bench as she spoke to Erica. "I will not come back." I understood her comment without translation reading her strong, broken face and her whispered determined statement.

We left there and went to one of the shelters that some churches run to give people supplies and rest until they were ready to run for the border.

We ate lunch with people there and met a man who had lost part of his foot jumping from a train in a previous effort to come to the U.S. He was on a Georgia bound train hoping to meet up with his friends in California. After the shelter, we stopped by the one place that was a sign of hope and possible improved future relations at the border.

We went to a coffee cooperative that had received large funding from several churches on the U.S. border. This money had been used to purchase some coffee roasters and grinders and packaging machines. The endeavor was run by people from a community in a southern Mexican state where exotic coffee is grown. They ship the coffee to their own processing plant at the border and don't have to sell it to big intermediaries. They are then able to process it and sell it for a good price as fair trade coffee. The churches help them to market their products. The profits realized by the growers in southern Mexico are enormous in comparison with the pittance that they make in the usual process that verges on slavery. The town in southern Mexico had been able to build a central water system and other community projects because of their prosperity. This is one example of what needs to happen on a large scale rather than moving manufacturing jobs from the U.S. to the border. People in the U.S. are left without work, and the Mexicans are paid a paltry sum. Nobody wins except the big box stores.

That whirlwind tour of the border with its double rows of high walls ended, and Erica brought me back. Before leaving Mexico, we walked along the twelve foot high steel walls to take a closer look. But we sensed that the closer we got to the walls, the more nervous the border guards became. We decided to back off and return home. Erica pointed out ranches where people set out water to help the Mexican migrants; ranches where several people were recently found dead in their tracks; and ranches where water lines for cattle troughs had been cut. Cattle died. Desperate people do desperate things. In the Diaspora, children died too. Further along, we stopped at Tombstone, Arizona for a thirst quencher. The town name reminded us that the desert has always been short on creature comforts. Finally, we arrived at her home. She prepared dinner for me and then resumed my education in international relations and/or U.S. xenophobia. We reminded ourselves once more that neither of us was an American Indian, so we were from families that immigrated to this country. Most of these foreigners were shunned, took low paying jobs and finally worked themselves up the ladder of success. Japanese Americans were put in concentration camps and the Navajo code talkers had to relearn their forbidden language to help the U.S. win the Pacific War. This last group still waits for acceptance and respect while treaties with them are disregarded. So what's new? So what have we learned? History repeats itself.

When we said goodbye I knew that very soon Erica was going back to El Salvador, and our next visit might be many years off. It occurred to me that our strong sense of connection, mutual respect and deep love was all built around Archbishop Romero. We were both joined at the heart with Romero as the spiritual bond. Over the years, we have shared letters and closely held values even when the miles between us were many.

Real friends don't have to live close to be very close. I drove away and I wondered. On that March day in 1946, when Winston Churchill gave the Iron Curtain Speech in Missouri with five year-old Kathy Dahl nearby, could he have ever dreamed or dared to hope that someday Europe would be without an Iron Curtain? Even as I left Tucson and saw Erica Dahl-Bredine's adobe disappearing in my rear view mirror, I dared to dream and hope. Someday North America, too, will exist without an iron curtain.

St. Bridget Parish

ARCHBISHOP JOHN MAY had allowed me to go to Notre Dame on loan. After two years, he called and told me not to sign another contract. "I need you in St. Louis." While it was hard to leave the people and the aura that is Notre Dame, it was music to my ears to have a bishop say that I was needed. That was the first time I had heard those words in my eighteen years of priestly service.

I said, "Where would you like me to go? I have a preference to return to the inner-city and black Catholics."

He said, "I don't know yet, but trust me and I will make you happy."

"Nobody makes me happy," I responded, "because I believe the saying of Abraham Lincoln that most people are as happy as they make up their minds to be." Archbishop May felt I would best serve as the pastor at St. Bridget Parish, which was in the middle of a huge vacant lot that had been the site of the ill-fated and infamous Pruitt-Igoe Housing Project. When it was imploded, it was the centerfold in *Life* Magazine.

There were still a few high-rise apartments six blocks from the church, as well as homes sprinkled among the crack houses and boarded up buildings. Most of all, there was a pride based on the legacy and imagination of a former pastor, Msgr. John Shocklee. He was loved and helped to keep St. Louis riot free after the murder of Dr. Martin Luther King, Jr. As a new pastor, there was no one with longer coat tails for me to ride. The parish still had a wonderful school and was continuing to give poor people the only gift that no one can take away — the gift of self-esteem based on educational success.

"BE SHEPHERDS LIVING WITH THE SMELL OF THE SHEEP"

Pope Francis said, "Small yet strong in the love of God, like Saint Francis of Assisi, all of us, as Christians, are called to watch over and protect the fragile world in which we live, and all its peoples." Ibid. *Evangelii Gaudium.* p. 155.

In the *South Side Journal* Lois Kendall wrote:

"Father Gerry Kleba, as he's affectionately known among his parishioners, learned some hard lessons in "reality" during his 10 years at the all-black, inner-city parish of Visitation. It helped prepare him for his current assignment at St. Bridget of Erin, which includes the area that used to be the Pruitt-Igoe Housing Projects.

Father Kleba has strong feelings about the "weed-infested acres" of what used to be Pruitt-Igoe. "The whole area is in violation of the city's noxious weed ordinances," he says. "It has grass and weeds over my head, and they didn't cut it once all summer. In two of those lots, they found dead bodies. You could put two giraffes and a mamba snake there, and Dana Brown could do his coffee commercials – you wouldn't know the difference between Kenya and Jefferson and Carr. It just goes on because in a poor neighborhood the assumption is 'those people like it ugly,' " Father Kleba says.

Father Kleba organized a neighborhood group which leased one of the abandoned acres for a community garden. "It took two months and a big hassle to convince the city to give us an attachment for the fire hydrant so we could water the garden. We beautified one acre; but I believe if they (the federal government) decided they wanted it, they would bulldoze our zinnias and zucchini in the middle of the summer. They wouldn't honor our agreement anymore than they honored the Indian treaties," Father Kleba says.

"That's all part of the real underlying problem – the feeling of being abandoned and messed over by the federal government," he says. "It took their homes to build the projects, then the projects were a nightmare, so they blew them up; so now they're back to no housing – they are powerless."

But Father Kleba refuses to throw up his hands and quit fighting, "I don't allow the phrase, 'What do you think they're going to do with that property?' When people ask me that, I say, 'They haven't done a damn thing with it in 13 years, what makes you think the people in the HUD office in Washington get up in the morning and say – 'I'm going to do something about Pruitt Igoe today!' What are we going to do about it?"

It's harder to build up a neighborhood today, Father Kleba says, because of a highly mobile society, coupled with increased unemployment, hunger and homelessness. "I just get so livid and so angry. Unemployment is a crisis, government housing programs are out of existence – no longer a priority for the country – out of that comes the resulting problems of alcoholism, drug addiction and crime," Father Kleba says.

The only way to realize any long-term good in a depressed neighborhood, Father Kleba says, is to build up the residents' self esteem and self worth. "It's just words, pious platitudes and brain massage if we decry the problems instead of working to remedy them," he says."

January 7, 1987. p. 3.

OMAR McROBERTS

Besides,
They'll see how beautiful I am
And be ashamed –
I too am America

Langston Hughes, *I too sing America*

THERE ARE ABOUT 600,000 CATHOLICS in St. Louis. I went through
the St. Louis Catholic seminary with only one black classmate during my
twelve years of schooling. What is the likelihood that I would be assigned
to a parish where that one friend from those years would be a member?
Whatever the statistical possibility, that is exactly what happened. I
reported in as pastor of St. Bridget parish and Bill McRoberts and his
wife, Minnie, were among the first to welcome me. The parish had a
wonderful reputation in this racially charged city as being a place where black
Catholics were proud and outgoing about their Catholic heritage. Much
of that had to do with a previous pastor who was an icon in the St. Louis
community, Msgr. John A. Shocklee.

If America has its very own cultural heritage, it is the music that
came out of the African-American experience. The clapping, drumming,
moaning and singing of the black slaves became the gospel, spiritual, blues,
and jazz that the whole world celebrates. So it is assumed in the black
church that music and singing is as precious as breathing. Choirs in church
are another manifestation of the Word of God alive and the Spirit moving
in the community. St. Bridget's had a good choir, but it was lacking in
instrumentation. There was a piano and organ, but no drums.

Omar McRoberts was a young teen who was comfortable sharing his
talents. His mother and father made their presence felt in serving the community. They were both dedicated to seeing all people develop to their
greatest potential. Bill ran an employment program in a depressed neigh-

borhood. Minnie was an employment specialist and social worker trying to get people on probation back on track in their lives. In that setting Omar and his younger sister, Ochanya, were expected to meet high standards and let their light shine before people so that they might see their good works and give glory to God.

Omar was ready to give glory to God by serving Mass and using his musical gifts as a drummer to enhance the music at St. Bridget's. The church did have a trap-set drummer, but not a conga player/percussionist. Omar played congas. Since the parish could not afford to buy congas, Bill carted the drums to church in his car and then took them home after Mass. This drudgery continued for many months in hot weather. In the steamy summertime, this required Bill to make two trips to and from church each week; one with the drums and the second with the family.

Bill stopped me to talk after Mass one Sunday. Omar accompanied Bill to my office, and I sat there clueless about the issue. "Gerry," this was casual rather than clerical, but we had known each other since we were seventeen years old. "I want to bring up something that might be a bit touchy."

"Sure, what's on your mind?"

"You're probably wondering why you don't see Omar playing drums on Sunday morning anymore. So I thought that we ought to have this meeting and tell you what's going on. Some time ago, the music director told Omar that he would be getting paid for his services here. We thought that he had gotten the approval from you, but you never said anything and no money was forthcoming." Bill always spoke eloquently and he continued. "Since we felt that Omar had been misled, his mother and I decided to pull Omar out of the band when the promise was not kept. No money, no music. We think this is a bad example for the choir director to set, whether or not he spoke out of turn. We would not allow Omar to be mishandled in that way."

I sighed and seethed over this situation. While I tried to be unemotional, I felt my anger showing on my face. It was not the choir director's place to offer pay to our volunteers when we already had a hard time meeting the payroll. Whether this was a conversation based on idle speculation or was a communication problem didn't really matter. Right now, Bill and Omar sat before me confused and disheartened. I sat there stunned by this revelation. I could not stand to have a fractured relationship with Bill and his family. I had known Bill longer than anyone in the parish. The relationship with him and his family was outstanding in every way.

I thought, "Thank God they came to talk, so this misunderstanding can be corrected sooner rather than later."

I hesitated, because I was taken aback by this discussion and the honesty of the challenge. I was certainly sympathetic to the question, but I was also aware of the tight budget in the parish. I tried to rephrase the question as they taught me in counseling class. That was to give me more time to fumble with a feeble response. "So you think that Omar should be paid like Oliver and Cathy. That's an understandable request, but you would have to agree that he is much younger than they are and still lives at home." I was stating the obvious trusting that the Holy Spirit would enlighten me. "Bill, if I paid Omar now, what do you think he would do with the money? Would he buy pizzas or cassettes of his favorite music?" I didn't really wait for a reply to the rhetorical questions because I knew the family and I imagined the response would be that he would save it for college. I continued, "Bill, I do pay those people you mentioned, but you have to know that neither of them are members of our church. They are employees. But you and your family are members of St. Bridget's, and you and your children all take advantage of a Catholic education. And you know that no one pays the entire cost of a Catholic school education, but that all of the families who send children there get underwritten by a large chunk of money. So the parish and the archdiocese support all the students in Catholic schools. One of the aspects of Catholic education is to teach children how to be servants and give back some of the gifts and talents that God has bestowed on them.

So, what if we said this? If you agree with all I have said, and it makes sense to you, we will have Omar continue to play for the church, and we won't pay him anything. It will be his return for God's given talents and the generous educational gift of the church. When Omar is older and needs the support of the church to continue his education, we will be there for him and pay him back later for the gifts he is giving us at this time." Wow, the Holy Spirit had been there on time! I was impressed with my response. I wondered whether Bill and Omar were.

Bill spoke up in his modulated but booming bass voice. Stroking his chin like the philosopher he was, he said, "Well Gerry, I didn't think that I was going to let you off that easy." He smiled warmly and continued, "But that really does make a lot of sense. I guess we'll just keep doing what we're doing, because I don't suppose you want to go out and buy some drums and cut down on the hauling job. If I were free on weekends, I could make some money hauling for others." It was a wonderful agreement and a delightful, honest exchange.

But I had to check with the drummer. "What do you think about this, little drummer boy?" In his typical eager, adult fashion Omar said, "Oh, it's fine with me. I enjoy playing and hope there's some money for me when I go to college."

Bill added, "Yes, both Omar and his dad can make a service contribution to the church that has given us so much." And they disappeared down the hall.

I settled back in my chair and realized that we had had a heartwarming conversation about church and values. It could as easily have become a budget busting shouting match. Bill and I had too much of a good history together for that to actually be the case. Little did I know that I would have some gut-wrenching times later on in my life in the housing projects. But God blesses us by keeping things secret and not passing out any crystal balls.

The music continued to improve in church, and Omar got better as a percussion player. He also grew in poise and dedication to service. This reached a pinnacle in high school when he was selected as the YMCA's Youth of the Year for the St. Louis area. During the banquet at the Hyatt-Regency, he gave an impressive talk with a world view that surpassed his years. When the talk was over, several of the people at my table were struck by Omar's maturity, command of language, and poise at the microphone. One of the executives from AT&T said to another from Monsanto, "Are you going to hire that kid this evening? If you don't, I think that I will." Omar did not get a job that night, but he did enjoy a prize of a three-week trip to the Y in Bogotá, Columbia, the sister Y to the one in St. Louis. Other parents might have been negative and frightened by the violence that pervaded, and still pervades that country. Indeed, one family did not allow their child to join the trip because of the violence. But Bill and Minnie trusted that adequate safety and contingency plans for escape were in place should violence break out.

After Omar graduated from Christian Brothers College High School, he won a scholarship to the University of Chicago. Now the time to pay the drummer who had worked so hard and believed in a promise had come. We also realized that Omar was not the only young person in the parish needing assistance to pay for college. We began a scholarship fund that helped people go to some prestigious distant schools and other people go to a junior college a few miles away. We also helped people go to technical school realizing that the skills to install and repair heating and air-conditioning were vital in St. Louis, a city where the temperature can vary over 100 degrees in one year.

All of the students had to submit a financial report, statement of need, previous semester's report card, and come before our committee. All of the students had to do that except for Omar. He had made his contribution, and now it was time for us to keep our part of the bargain. While he never made an application, and in fact, did not meet the financial need or residency requirements to apply for a scholarship, every semester for four years we sent Omar a check for $1,000.00. When he concluded his studies after four years, I sat in the auditorium next to his grandmother and was stunned to hear him introduced as the valedictorian of the class. I held his grandmother back as she fell forward with her hands over her mouth in shock. His girl friend, Shellie, was also in awe. We didn't get to see Bill and Minnie, because they had choice parent seats in the Rockefeller Chapel where the actual event took place. Later on, they testified that they had not been informed in advance. Maybe Omar wasn't either and that is why so much of his talk reminded me of the award winning speech from that night at the YMCA dinner. The YMCA winner received a trip to Columbia; the valedictorian received a trip to Harvard University for a full ride to a doctoral degree. Thank God, Omar had not wasted his money on pizza.

After helping the family move Omar's stuff home, I took him out to lunch as a graduation present. He owed me one more favor. "Omar, what would you think about spending the afternoon with me? We will go to visit some of the folks who fund our scholarship program. You can thank them and tell them your story." He eagerly agreed. "Well I have a question for you right now. Tell me what it was like getting that $1,000.00 each semester?"

"Well, Father the truth is that the $1,000.00 helped me to buy books, supplies and food. I was blessed with abundant support—including several scholarships and undergraduate research fellowships. The additional $1,000 further insured that I would not need to get a job, which surely would have distracted me from my studies. That's what the money meant to me."

We visited one of our donors and he gave me the impression that he was always eager to fund someone who was a Harvard candidate. He found it harder to understand that with a pittance, he could also help keep a student in a community college or a technical school and that was important too. When he expressed some doubt, I thought that I would take the risky step of embarrassing him. He had helped us generously, so I didn't really see that as a concern.

"Mr. Lohr," I said, knowing full well that he made his money in the beer distributorship that he owned, "does your business depend more on a sociologist or on a person who knows how to keep the refrigeration up in a blast of St. Louis summer?"

He smiled and immediately got the drift of my question. He continued to fund us with handsome amounts of his beer money.

Omar went off to Harvard and continued to thrive there. We saw him very little at St. Bridget's, so I decided that I owed him a visit. I love history anyway, and I had not been to Boston for years. One day he met me at the Cambridge Station. It was great to hug him, look into his eyes, and size up his fuller physique. He still displayed that warm and always authentically unassuming smile.

"Well where do you want to go?" he asked as we watched the traffic streaming by.

"What do you think? I came this far so that you could show me Harvard."

We crossed the street when the light changed, and he ushered me into the John Harvard Brewing Co. "Well, here we are," he announced as he sauntered up to the bar.

"Here we are," I said as I mimicked him with some skepticism. "This is a bar, I thought that there was a school here somewhere," I quizzed.

"A school, there's a school here somewhere? I thought that this is where I won the scholarship." We laughed. It was the comfort level of old times. He was the age of his dad and I when we went to college together. But now he was here as a very astute adult who would never try to dazzle me with his brilliance. We had a beer and then we crossed the street in the other direction so that he could take me to his office.

After my campus tour, we stopped at the store next to the brewery. This was the Harvard Bookstore. He asked me if he could buy me a gift as a memento of my Harvard visit. When I consented, he bought me a t-shirt, but then we moved to the bookshelves. He picked up a book, seemingly at random, and asked, "What would you think if I bought you this one?"

I had never seen it before, and there was no indication on the cover that this was a best-seller. It was a collection of short stories, essays and poetry by black, male authors. I paged through it and then noticed in the table of contents that Omar had written several of the poems in the book. One was a poem about his father. "There is nothing in the whole store that I would treasure more." His father and I had come a long way together, and I had to claim a part of Omar as my own. As we stood at the checkout line, I hoped that Omar would always be my son. I missed his Harvard graduation, but I was with him in spirit.

Some years later I went back to Chicago. This time I got into the University Church for a ceremony. Omar and Shellie were married there. Now he teaches at the University of Chicago, and they have a daughter and a son.

I have often pondered the question of how much faith Bill and Omar and I had on that Sunday morning when we shook hands and made a deal. How much did we trust God and each other? Bill and Omar had to believe that my word was good. In a world where priests are transferred, they had to believe that I would still be at St. Bridget's when the time came to make those delayed payments. Both they and I had to believe that our impoverished church would have money to pay scholarships to Omar and to dozens of others. I doubt that the children of Omar and Shellie live or worship in the shadows of high-rise housing projects. I imagine that they are tempted by many consumerist, instant gratification values. But I hope and pray, and I truly believe that when they are teens they, like their father, will march to a different drummer.

JOHN O'LEARY

"Noble hearts do crack. Health, at every level is easily lost.
But hearts are also strong and life resilient. The darkness comes
for its untimely visitation; light also is given in
and through the cracks."
Robert F. Morneau – *Mantra for the Midnight*

THE FOOD PANTRY AND THE CLOTHING STORE at St. Bridget's Parish were busy all week long serving the poor. It was even busy on Sunday when we were supposedly not open. That was the day when our sister parishes in wealthier parts of the St. Louis area made deliveries and re-plenished the supplies. One of the faithful supporters of this life-saving effort was St. Clement of Rome Parish. Dennis O'Leary drove his van that Sunday stacked with cereal and canned goods in the rear and stuffed with youngsters in the seats. When the groceries were unloaded and many of them sorted and shelved, Dennis searched me out in the parish house having lunch after the Sunday Masses.

"Father, I hate to impose on you on a busy Sunday, but would you have time to take us on a little trip around the neighborhood and show these kids what life is like among the poor? They come from such privilege and they're good kids who want to help, but they don't have any idea how blessed they really are. And when I say that, I know that my own kids are spoiled, so I'm not just talking about other families. In fact, I need to have the tour myself."

There was no way for me to refuse such an honest request and besides that our parish had been dependent on St. Clement's since before I arrived as pastor. "Sure, let me finish here in a minute and I'll be out to give you the tour." Before leaving the street by the church, I told them a bit about the racial rancor that has divided St. Louis since the time of the Civil War. Missouri was the only state that didn't secede from the Union,

but still was a slave owning state. "Besides that we are the city where the Dred Scott decision was made that contributed to the Civil War. So we have a kind of split personality, historically speaking," I said. "Does anybody know what that means?"

Several teens had some vague answers, but I now, at least, had them involved in the conversation and they would now ask questions rather than just listen to me talk. I pointed out the high-rise housing projects, how close they were to one another and how little play area there was for the kids. We talked about how many acres there were for hundreds of people and how many of the kids in the van had a single family house standing on one acre by itself. It was eye-opening for them. We saw glass in the gutters, litter in the streets and homeless people gathered around 55-gallon drums being used as fire pits. In the heated van wearing our winter coats, we reflected on the attraction of a few blazing logs. People came together around the flickering firelight for a bit of thawing warmth. These chilled residents' spirits were also warmed by the booze in brown paper bags being passed around. We saw dilapidated brick structures where some people made a living by knocking the cement off the bricks so the bricks could be resold. In other places, people lived by stealing and selling the bricks that were then used in the construction of mega mansions in other parts of the area, even as far away as Houston.

Then we came to a neighborhood where the century old Falstaff Brewery building, which had been vacant for decades, was being rehabbed into condos. Some of the homes in the neighborhood were also being remodeled. "What do you think is going on here?" I asked.

"It looks like its being rehabbed, but who would want to live in an area like this?" came a cynical voice from the rear. Since I was in the front and the seats had high backs, I didn't see the speaker.

"Well there is some truth to what you say. A big developer is making apartments out of that derelict brewery. Some residents are working on their homes, but that work is too expensive for most, so the area is only getting half improved. Most of the folks here can't afford to do much to improve their property. Even if the owners had the money, most contractors don't want to come into the area. They are afraid that they will be ripped off. Either the bills won't get paid, or their trucks and tools will be stolen while they are in the house working. That makes it difficult for people to stay here even if they have some money and would like to upgrade their homes.

Another part of the problem is that the rehabs attract a lot of city building inspectors into the area to oversee the new work. While they are here, they see a lot of code violations everywhere. Some of these blocks haven't had a building inspector on them for ten years and now the inspector writes a code violation citation and gives the homeowner sixty days to get repairs made. It's impossible either because folks have no money or because the repairmen won't come into the neighborhood to work. It's a lose/lose situation. It makes it impossible to improve the area unless all the poor people lose their homes and become homeless."

I thought that was enough of an education for students who had only come to sort cans and not to take Urban Studies 101 on a bright Sunday afternoon when the football game was on television. I directed Dennis to drive back to the parish. As I was getting out, I thanked everyone for their continuing interest in St. Bridget's as well as their general concern for the poor. I said my goodbyes while encouraging the students who went to excellent private Catholic high schools to continue their good work. At the same time, Dennis got out of the van to shake my hand and thank me again. As he squeezed my hand he said, "Thanks for the tour and for the education. If there is ever a way that I can help you, let me know. You just have to know that I am an attorney, and I'm not much good for anything." He handed me his business card as he gave me a wide, warm Irish smile. He got back in the van and they all rode into the sunset toward the wealthy western part of our city.

I'm usually good at remembering generous offers to help, but I didn't need an elephant's memory to recall Dennis O'Leary's offer when I got a call two weeks later. Mrs. Cassidy was the feeble, elderly owner of a four family flat one block away from the brewery redevelopment. I brought her Holy Communion regularly in her cluttered apartment. Hers was the only occupied one of the four in the building. The reasons why the others were vacant were many. First, she was afraid that she might get some tenant who would bring in drugs and gangs. Second, she didn't have the money to fix up the apartment that needed the most repairs. Also, she was leery about a tenant that might report the mess to the city inspectors. And finally, she was old and tired. She had enough to do to take care of her personal needs.

Now the city inspectors had given her a list of code violations. She had sixty days to get the violations fixed. If she didn't comply, the building would be condemned and she would be homeless. Her health was not good to start with and now this situation was complicating her congestive heart and her high blood sugar. And worst of all, she had no family or any place else to go. If she could go somewhere better, she would have done that. After her husband died years ago, she had been alone. She was faced with a sixty-day edict: comply or be homeless. She faced the very horror I had reported to the students during our tour two Sundays earlier.

I had an immediate idea. She had to appear in housing court. Dennis, that "useless" lawyer, had offered help as he squeezed his card into my hand while thanking me for the lecture on wheels. I would call Dennis and see if he was serious. Dennis was practically gleeful that I called. I told him that we would have to visit Mrs. Cassidy in her home. I thought that would give him a better feel for the needy folks he would be speaking for in court. I was also conscious that downtown lawyers usually dressed in nice threads and that roaches and other critters were not strangers to homes in the community. First, I was going to tell him to dress down, but I thought that Mrs. Cassidy deserved to have a lawyer come to her in the same way they came to the help of his regular clientele.

When Dennis arrived at my house, I gave him the background on the situation and how these things usually worked with people. As we met with Mrs. Cassidy, Dennis displayed the same warmth that I had seen in every situation I had been in with him. Dennis studied the citation from the City of St. Louis. It required more than a quick perusal, because he had never seen a document like this. Poverty law was not the stuff that made downtown law firms prosperous. We had a delightful visit with Mrs. Cassidy. As Dennis was driving me back to the parish he said, "I'll learn a lot studying this case, but it will be fun and worthwhile. Is there anything else that I can do for you today?"

I explained that my car was in the shop and I had some errands to run. "Are you going to be at your office downtown for the rest of the day? If so, could I take you to your office and then use your car for the afternoon? I could then pick you up at five o'clock."

Dennis said, "Sure, I don't see why not, I wasn't going anywhere this afternoon. Now I have some homework to do on the city housing code anyway."

I took him back to work, and in the process of driving the neighborhood, picked up a nail in the front tire of his car; or maybe it was glass, there was plenty of each to go around. With the AAA's assistance, I got the spare mounted and my work done. I picked Dennis up at his office. I told him that the nail in his tire was his reward for being a Good Samaritan to an old lady in need. Knowing that he had a good sense of humor, I told him to "remember, no good deed ever goes unpunished." Dennis was a fast learner. He was quickly becoming aware that it's harder and more costly to live and work in a poor community than in an affluent one.

Dennis maneuvered through housing court and got Mrs. Cassidy an extension of two more months to make the needed repairs. Then he talked to a retired builder in St. Clement of Rome Parish. Ed Meiners was the personification of St. Joseph the carpenter and the St. Vincent de Paul Society. He looked at Mrs. Cassidy's building and started to take measurements and make a needs assessments. What about the roof, the heat, the wiring, the plumbing, the brick work, the front porch steps, the windows and doors? Every aspect of the structure was scrutinized under his eagle eye. The project was enormous, and the cost was way beyond Mrs. Cassidy's pension and social security. Ed Meiner thought two things: "If a task is difficult, it ought to be done." Secondly, "people who had money had money to help those who had big needs and little money." Ed rallied the forces, mustered the volunteers and invaded Mrs. Cassidy's house, tearing it apart to put it back together in better shape. It seemed that half of St. Clement's parish was involved in the work. The building inspectors couldn't believe their eyes. Mrs. Cassidy, this humble grandma sweetheart, loved seeing her workers in jeans and her lawyer in his "downtown" duds coming to work for her. This was like Habitat for Humanity without the label.

As the rehab was progressing apace with the brewery renovation work across the street, the winds of January began to blow. The St. Vincent de Paul Conference at St. Clement Parish asked me to bring my gospel choir out to their parish to sing while I celebrated the Mass in honor of Martin Luther King Day. That was the least we could do. It required some planning to transport singers and instruments to the western suburbs since most of our people didn't have cars. It was a minor task to repay Ed Meiners' work crew as well as keeping the connection between our two churches vibrant and growing. Besides, not all the churches that we partnered with had enough of a social conscience to even know that it was Martin Luther King Day, much less highlight it in their affluent white parish. Not only was there was no interest, it was discouraged to have any pepper in the salt in these racist places. White flight was about separating the races. This also meant economic divisions were created, although that was seldom mentioned. Despite all of that, St. Clements was welcoming. They prepared a nice social after Mass so that the choir could have fellowship with their people.

I went to St. Clement's by myself that Sunday, because I had somewhere to go after Mass. When I got out of my car and reached for my extra long vestments out of the backseat, Rita Andres came over to greet me. If Ed Meiners was "Mr." St. Vincent de Paul in their parish, then Rita was "Mrs." After welcoming me she said, "Do you know what you are supposed to preach today?"

I was a bit taken aback by the question thinking that I ought to know fifteen minutes before Mass, but also thinking that they did invite a black choir to sing on Martin Luther King Day, not on Flag Day. That should have been enough of a hint for me. I ventured to say, "I guess I'm supposed

to preach on Catholic social justice issues and the life of Dr. King." I think
I ended with a bit of a treble question mark in my voice.

"No, I don't think so. Yesterday Dennis O'Leary's little boy, John,
was playing with matches and burned down the house and got seriously
burned in the blaze. He's in the burn unit at St. John's and you should
preach on why bad things happen to good people."

Thinking about the fire and the new preaching theme sent cold
chills down my back. With tears in my eyes, I reached out to hug Rita. I
was in a numb stupor. "I can't believe it," I muttered.

"Last night we had a prayer service at church and Dennis talked
to everyone. He tried to calm us. He asked us to pray and just hope with
the family. He was the steadiest and most focused one in the church.
Throughout all of this, his son John is hanging on by the tiniest thread
of life."

I was still a statue on the parking lot with my vestments dragging on
the blacktop. If I could have moved, I would have gotten in my car and
returned to the hood. This was a nightmare. But now I had five minutes
to decide what to preach on the topic "Why bad things happen to good
people."

In my preaching that day I made a confession. I told people that
when I was about seven years old on a boring Sunday afternoon I decided
that it would be safe and exciting to get some matches, light the bathroom
toilet paper, slowly feed it off the roll in the tile wall and have my own
small camp fire. I was certain that all the water close at hand would allow
me to control things. My mother smelled the smoke as the hem of the
bathroom curtain was singed by the fire. She was able to control the fire
with the water in the bathroom. Finally, she burned my seat bottom with
a few well targeted swats. I was saved from John O'Leary's fate, but I
certainly understood a small boy's infatuation with fire. My blessing was
that I wasn't in a garage with gasoline cans nearby.

The people of St. Clements certainly needed the upbeat, energetic hope that is typical of gospel music. We all needed to be assured by
"What a Friend We Have in Jesus." We also needed to hear "We Shall

Overcome" with its hopeful refrain "Do Not Be Afraid." Whatever errand had prompted me to come to St. Clements in my own car was superseded by the need to go to St. John's Hospital and be a prayerful support to the O'Leary family. There was a huge cohort in the waiting room outside the burn unit and there I got the story straight. John had been playing with matches in the garage attached to the house. The gas can for the lawn mower exploded and spewed flames all over his body. His parents were out, but his older brother Jim got him and threw him in the snow in the yard, saving his life.

When the ambulance arrived, the EMTs questioned whether they could get him into the ambulance alive. They doubted that he would live to be moved to the emergency room at the hospital. Later the doctors questioned whether he could live through the stress and agony of being moved upstairs to the burn unit. At every step of the way, the odds were impossible and the faith of the family and the larger community kept John alive. Dennis and Susan, the parents, had to be like the parents in the gospel who said, "Yes Lord, I believe, help my unbelief."

John lived, progressing with excruciating pain. He had the support of a platoon of doctors and prayers, nurses and prayers, therapists and prayers, bathers and prayers, feeders and prayers, parents, brothers, sisters and extended family that just wouldn't go away. Susan, John's beautiful mother, was always there. Whenever I went to visit, I saw Susan looking like she had just come from a cover-girl photo-shoot at *Vogue*. I'm sure that she had a hand in encouraging the staff in whatever way that she could. Susan was going to be at the hospital as a picture of life, hope, beauty and love. God is all of those and in this situation Susan was the face of God. If "beauty will save the world," as Dostoyevsky said, Susan was a saving presence at her son's side in the hospital.

I would go to the hospital to pray and visit with Susan and John when that was appropriate. I prayed in the hospital waiting room with whoever was gathered. At other times, I would go down in the hospital chapel to pray in solitude. I was never there to get in the way. I have always been confident that God hears prayers and directs their fruits properly whether the petitioner is near or far. Many years later, as I was visiting with John, he said that he was always excited to hear me come in to visit and pray with his mom. I was delighted, but I always thought that he was comatose. With all the bandages, tubes, and tracheotomy he was unable to see, talk or move for several months.

All this time while the O'Leary's home was being rebuilt, they were never without a house. There was always someone in their parish going on a winter vacation or a snowbird couple living in the south. They gave their homes to the O'Leary's so that the other children in the family got to school and had meals together. Dennis had saved a house for Mrs. Cassidy; now God was providing a house for the O'Leary's. They received home cooked meals delivered daily from dozens of fellow parishioners. They never had to phone in an order.

The lifesaving procedures continued ceaselessly. The promise of recovery was moment-to-moment at first, and then hour-to-hour. If John survived, the question about his percentage of activity and mobility was always there. He had one obvious incredible blessing out of the whole disaster. He suffered very little injury on his face or hair, sparing him horrible disfigurement. However, his hands were severely burned and all of his fingers gone to below the middle knuckle. All of the skin over ninety percent of his body was fried and suffered from severe scar tissue. This meant that the skin would never reproduce and skin grafts would have to be performed regularly as he grew so that the skin could expand as his skeleton expanded. The problems were massive, the progress was incremental. The amount of inner work that little John, his parents and all who loved him had to do was beyond my imagining.

One of the people who lightened John's burden was a great national celebrity and all-time St. Louis hero, Jack Buck, the voice of the St. Louis Cardinals and many Super Bowls and World Series games. Jack made it a practice to visit sick kids, and soon John O'Leary was on the top of his list. When the mellifluous voice of KMOX, the 'Voice of St. Louis,' floated into the burn unit, no one needed to question his identity. "How you doing, kid? I'm Jack Buck." Once Jack made his presence felt, he did not go away. Visit after visit, game broadcast after broadcast, Jack urged John to keep fighting. He then went on a mission to assist John's recovery.

Jack would tell John's tragic story to the St. Louis baseball team as well as sports people across the country and arrange for them to autograph a baseball for John's recovery. Jack started his therapy by mailing John a baseball autographed by Cardinal Manager Whitey Herzog, telling John in a note that if he wanted a second autographed baseball he had to write a thank you note to the player or personality signing the first ball. John looked at his stubs of fingers and asked his mom, "What is with this request? He expects the impossible." For John, with such severely injured fingers, this was an immense challenge.

With his parent's help and encouragement, he would get the impossible accomplished. A scribbled and barely legible thank you note was submitted, and Jack sent a second autographed baseball, this time signed by Ozzie Smith with words of encouragement. The project continued, with John continuing to receive a ball with each thank- you note returned. When the season ended, he was the proud owner of sixty-one baseballs and the proud author of 61 legible thank-you notes, crafted in response to Jack's challenge.

When John graduated from St. Louis University, Jack presented him with a gift. When John unwrapped the package, he discovered that he was the proud recipient of a Waterford Crystal Baseball from Cooperstown. It had been engraved for Jack Buck when he was inducted into the announcers' wing of the Baseball Hall of Fame. It's priceless, one of a kind. It was given to John with the simple note,"This is important to me; I hope it is important to you." Jack referred to John as "the gutsiest, most courageous, toughest kid I have known in my whole life." John had one more baseball, a Hall of Fame ball, as the pinnacle of his collection. As a college graduate, John wrote one more thank you letter to Jack Buck. He did it quite quickly and proficiently on a computer.

John, now in his thirties, is married to his beautiful wife, Beth, who is a physical therapist. They have four children. John's business changed several years ago from a construction contractor rehabilitating homes to an inspirational speaker rehabilitating and motivating lives. He has spoken to enthusiastic audiences ranging from groups of 5 through 5,000 in 47 states and 4 foreign countries including Australia and China. John spends a good deal of his time as a motivational speaker. No one has deeper roots in the field or knows more from personal experience than John O'Leary does.

— "Unless the Lord builds the house, in vain do the builders labor."

Ps 127:1

FROM JOHN'S FATHER, DENNIS O'LEARY

Gerry, sorry for the delay in getting back to you. We enjoyed the trip down "memory lane." Most of my suggested changes are on the last two pages. I hope this is of some help. I will look forward to being one of your first customers.

St. Joseph Parish

ST. JOSEPH PARISH IS IN CLAYTON, an old, upscale suburb of Saint Louis. This setting placed me in the midst of the rich and powerful people whom I had frequently perceived as the 'enemy' during my many years in poor parishes. Slowly I found that I had a lot to learn about well-to-do people and that many of these deeply committed, faith-filled people were open to being challenged and were all ears when I shared stories of my inner-city exploits. Some of them became invaluable supporters of Catholic education in St. Bridget's, and others joined in an ecumenical endeavor to help build Habitat for Humanity housing. Subsequently, they have built eighteen homes, and I am considered the unofficial chaplain for Habitat given the fact that I have blessed many clusters of new homes. I also had entre into the parish because of my history teaching at the University of Notre Dame. Those connections, along with celebrating Mass for the Saint Louis chapter of the alumni club, opened more doors and hearts and homes to me. As I was discovering that affluent people are not the enemy, I also became aware that there are more kinds of poverty than just financial need.

"BE SHEPHERDS LIVING WITH THE SMELL OF THE SHEEP"

Pope Francis said, "Dialogue and friendship with the children of Israel (Jews) are part of the life of Jesus' disciples. The friendship — which has grown between us makes us bitterly and sincerely regret the terrible persecutions which they have endured, and continue to endure, especially those that have involved Christians." Ibid. *Evangelii Gaudium.* p. 171.

In the *Saint Louis Post-Dispatch* Bill McClellan said: "**Couple embraced the world after they found each other.**

In 1925, a fire caused heavy damage at St. Joseph's Catholic Church in Clayton. Adolph Gutman, a Jewish businessman who owned a nearby department store, delivered a large check to the priest. I think Clayton needs a Catholic church, Gutman said.

If the church can ever do anything for you, said Father Victor Stepka. The businessman gave him a quizzical look. If your kids want to get married at the church, there is always a place for them, said the priest. Both men laughed.

That is the story that has been handed down. Handed down and nearly forgotten until this summer, when David Gutman, Adolph's grandson, married Susie Ziervogel at St. Joseph's. David was 56. Susie was 40. It was the first marriage for each.

Before Susie met David, she was doing OK. She worked at a fast-food restaurant for eight years, and then she got a job at a grocery store as a bagger. A very nice job. Plus, she was living alone. So, she had reason to feel good about herself. She had been a Special School District student in the days before mainstreaming came into vogue. As a developmentally disabled kid, she had gone to school with other developmentally disabled kids.

When she was 27, she went to Columbia, Mo., to live in a group home for developmentally disabled people. When she returned to St. Louis three years later, she enrolled in a Life Skills program. As its name suggests, its goal is to teach people how to live independently. Which is exactly what Susie was doing. Working and living alone.

David was out in the world, too. He lived with his stepmother, but he worked at the St. Louis County Election Board. He started working there in 1966. He hardly ever missed a day. As of last week, he had accumulated 1,897.9 hours of sick time. It is, people say, an unofficial record.

He was a cheerful sort, even before he met Susie. He'd show up every morning with a bag of pretzels, or a box of bagels. Cheerful and happy, but sheltered. Didn't get out much. Absolutely unstylish. Went from home to work, and work to home. His only diversion was bowling.

So that is how Susie and David met. At a bowling alley. I talked to Susie this week, and I asked how long it took her to realize that David was Mr. Right. She laughed.

"Second frame," she said. "Right away."

David was just as smitten. David and Susie become inseparable.

Susie was like a teen-ager, so much in love. David was changed too. For one thing, he was going out. Work was still important, but now there were other things, as well. He was going to restaurants. He was planning trips. He even became a little conscious of his clothes. Most noticeably, he started wearing dark socks.

David and Susie were married this past July, July 10, to be exact. Father Gerry Kleba of St. Joseph's and Rabbi Joseph Rosenbloom of Temple Emanuel co-officiated.

These were two people who had thought they would never find someone," Father Kleba said. "And then to find each other. They were just aglow. We are all broken and fragile people, but these two people came together to make a perfect whole."

Rabbi Rosenbloom said, "If you were writing a novel, you couldn't do better than this."

In fact, the emotions were so high that the wedding party had a difficult time getting through the rehearsal. When it came time for David to acknowledge his love, he was crying.

Father Kleba was prepared for the actual service. As the ceremony approached the point when the bride and groom would have to speak, the priest said, "In the 157-year history of this church, we have had a number of double-ring ceremonies. This is our first double-hankie ceremony." Then he pulled out two handkerchiefs, and handed one to Susie and one to David.

The couple honeymooned at Disney World. They were soon taking other trips. Kansas City, Chicago, even Quebec. So many places to see now that they each had somebody with whom to see these places.

Last Saturday, they went to a movie. The weather was bad, and they came out in the cold and maybe the cold triggered David's asthma attack, but he suddenly fell to his knees in the snow. "Are you all right?" asked his wife.

He looked up at her, and said, "I love you, Susie, and I always will," and then he fell headfirst into the snow.

"I love you, too, David," said Susie.

Rabbi Rosenbloom prepared the eulogy, "Your loss is tragic," he wrote. "A good man, a wonderful relationship, cut off all too soon, too suddenly – but your love, your memories, will live on." Yes, that was the tone he wanted.

His eulogy went over well, and Susie understood exactly what the rabbi meant. A love story is never judged by its length."

January 10, 1999. p. 1 D.

CLAIR and JAXON SMITH

"Home is the place where, when you have to go there,
they have to take you in."
Robert Frost, *The Death of the Hired Man*

I FINISHED BLESSING THE YOUNGSTERS who were going to the Children's Liturgy of the Word and I turned my back to go to the priest's chair for the scripture readings. Little did I know that I was being followed as I ascended the steps on that Sunday morning. But when I adjusted my vestments and sat down there was a tiny speck of a six-year-old girl with golden locks that reminded me of a children's tale by the same name. She sat in the chair next to mine since one of the scheduled Mass servers hadn't shown up. She seemed quite comfortable being on display in front of hundreds of worshipers at the 10 o'clock Mass. I had never seen her before, and I didn't know who she was, but she was beautiful and winsome, and I didn't want to shoo her away. As we both settled into our chairs I was distracted from hearing the Bible reading as I tried to understand how she happened to be with me on the platform in front of the church. I never imagined that this moment would be so life-altering and memorable.

As the lector read, "A Reading from the Book of the Prophet Isaiah," I pondered the situation that was unfolding under my nose and the presence of this confident tyke at my side. At St. Joseph Parish in Clayton, Missouri, the Sunday school class for the youngsters was conducted by two dedicated teenage girls, Laura Dickmann and Katie Swetye. They were so vibrant on Sundays and so faithful to the preparation time on Tuesday afternoons after school. They were models for the adults, especially for the parents, who always seemed to take for granted their efforts and fidelity.

After I finished the opening prayer at Mass, I invited the children to come forward along with the catechists, Katie and Laura, and some parents who assisted as teacher aides. I blessed the gathering and then they proceeded out the side front door and descended the steps to the church basement. On this particular lovely autumn Sunday when the sun was streaming through the "life of Joseph" stained glass windows that decorated the north and south walls, I issued the invitation and about twenty children came to the front of the side aisle. I blessed them, and they processed from the body of the church to the lower level. Then I turned to go to the celebrant's chair in the center of the sanctuary along with the server who accompanied me. As I was settling into my place, I noticed the precious girl with golden blond hair walking the steps behind me. Apparently, she had hesitated in joining the others when I issued the invitation and, since she was shorter than Zacheus and had no tree to climb, she arrived in the front of the church after the other children had disappeared. Since she saw no other children, she presumed that she was to accompany me to the top of the platform in the center facing the four hundred worshipers.

As I was settling into my chair, she seemed equally comfortable getting into her seat with her feet dangling without touching the floor. She seemed at ease knowing her place, but I knew that I had never seen the girl before. She was such a little princess and Goldilocks all rolled into one gorgeous child that it was hard for me to imagine that she might be a regular at St. Joseph's whom I had somehow overlooked. I recalled a line from the musical, *Les Miserables*, "To love another person is to see the face of God."

I was sitting down with her next to me almost as if we had rehearsed our roles. I was in the center and the princess was on my right. She seemed comfortable enough in a place of prominence, but I imagined she must be a bit nervous and self-conscious. She exuded such ease that I was overly solicitous, but as the lector proclaimed the first lesson from the Hebrew scripture, I leaned down and whispered, "Welcome, what's your name," trusting that my warmth would disarm any hint of stage fright that she might suffer.

She looked up and in a tiny wisp of breath responded, "Clair."

I was impressed that she was totally unfazed by the audience. I continued anyway, "Sometimes when we are in front of such a big crowd, we all do better if we hold hands. Can we hold hands today"?

She looked up with a radiant smile and she reached up and placed her tiny soft hand in my large hand. She was totally comfortable and seemed to fit the gospel description of Nathaniel, a girl "without guile." Her lips were so pink and her complexion was so creamy that she looked like a big version of a china doll. The psalm for the day was Psalm 80 with the repeated verse, "O God let your face shine on us that we might be saved." I'm not sure that I ever appreciated the line before, but when I looked at Clair's poised calmness, I knew what God's shining face looked like. She was the portrait of innocence.

As the second reading from Paul's epistle was proceeding, I noticed a trim, mustached thirty-something gentleman creeping up the side aisle to the front of church. He was moving from one radiator to the next up to the front trying to hide his movements. I assumed that this must be Clair's dad both from his look of cautious and tentative embarrassment and his movement that was not a part of the liturgy. He was trying to be inconspicuous but at the same time determined to achieve his goal and retrieve his daughter.

The choir was beginning the Alleluia and the petrified gentleman had reached the front of the church on the side with the pulpit. I whispered to my new friend, "Clair, I have to go now, and it would be best for you not to stay here by yourself. Would you like to come with me to the man in front of church?" She nodded in agreement, processed down the steps and walked hand in hand with me over to the pulpit. Her dad met us and whisked her into his arms and then returned to his place by the center aisle, radiant with relief. I had the sense that all of this personal commotion for me had transpired largely unnoticed while people were changing their posture from standing to sitting and singing and listening at the same time. I surmised that few if any noticed the addition of this charming munchkin to the Sunday celebration.

Whatever the general tenor of the congregation and whether or not they even noticed this child, I suspected that after a scant five minutes, I was attached to this Clair as closely as Francis of Assisi was attached to his Clare. If she was a mere blip on the mental radar for the people assembled at St. Joseph's Church that Sunday, she was unforgettable for me.

After I finished reading the gospel and was to begin my preaching, I made a pastoral decision that I would say nothing about Clair's visit to the presider's chair. First, I didn't think most people had noticed anything strange about the liturgy that day since the visitor was so small and unobtrusive. Secondly, and much more importantly, I didn't want Clair or her parents to be embarrassed. Either they were new to the parish, and in that case I surely didn't want to scare them off, or they were guests staying in town and I wanted them to sense our warmth. In either case, it would not be appropriate to highlight what some might consider a misstep. It seemed clear that Clair was comfortable in a leading role, and it was not my position to downgrade her to a supporting role. In my mind, she won the Oscar for her disarming charm and warmth in stealing my heart with the small part she played that Sunday.

I have no memory of what I preached about that day and even less of a notion as to whether I touched anyone with the message of God's love. However, I do know that I was touched deeply by the message of God's love in the Sunday surprise of Clair with the beautiful face, the tiny voice, the luxurious hair, the soft trusting hand, the confident step, the proud seating and the gentle poise of this Godsend of loveliness who warmed my heart so profoundly in that unexpected instant. The surprise of the moment along with her confidence, her fragile luminescence and the peachy radiance that she embodied took my breath away. She had stolen my heart or, rather, pilfered it; she did it so coyly. Additionally, it is proper to say her presence filled me with reverence, awe and wonder at her comfort and ease in God's house. Maybe, it was even bliss. And in a moment she was gone into the arms of a stranger who turned out to be her dad. She disappeared into the crowd as mysteriously as she had appeared in the first place. Who was she and why had I not seen her before? Would her family bring her to the coffee and donut time after Mass? Certainly they would, or that was certainly my hope. After all, what kid doesn't like donuts?

Sadly I was wrong. They didn't bring her, and I didn't see them next Sunday either. Maybe they were out of town visitors and she had appeared to light up my life for a nanosecond like the exciting appearance of a shooting star in the midnight darkness. I was scared by the sadness that seared my broken heart over this special moment that ended in a blink. Would this hand holding ray of sunshine reappear? The next week I wrote an article in the St. Joseph Parish bulletin, *Oh Where, Oh Where is Little Clair?*

I didn't have to hire a private investigator however, because Clair appeared while I was standing and greeting people at the end of Mass the very next Sunday. As I was talking to people, I saw this apparition of Goldilocks walking past. Without missing a syllable of my adult conversation I reached down and grabbed her arm as she walked by. "Clair," I almost shouted in glee, but I restrained myself, "Please, wait here a minute; I need to see you." With that her parents noticed and stepped aside out of the exit line into the corner of the vestibule. I was thrilled to see Claire again and know that her family had not been merely passing through on vacation.

Her name was Clair Smith. I also met her parents, Ed and Sue and her younger brother, Jaxon. They had just moved into the parish because Ed's job as a sales rep had brought them to St. Louis. They were in a bit of a hurry that Sunday also, but I told them that they were just in time to be included in our new parish directory that was about to go to the printer on Monday. "All I need is for you to bring a family photo to the rectory first thing in the morning." That photo along with their registration information would allow us to include them and make the book complete.

Sue was quick to explain, "We'd love to be included," she assured me, "but all of our stuff is in boxes and I don't know where we can lay our hands on the right box that contains a good family picture."

I was not to be deterred and so I assured her. "You're in luck, because you have just joined a full service parish. I will be at your home at two o'clock this afternoon and I will take your picture with my camera. Now you can't beat that for service." I wanted the directory to be complete and to include this family that had captured my heart.

I arrived at their house just as I had promised. Clair quickly answered the door before I even pressed the doorbell. Her first question was, "Do you want to come out in the backyard and meet our dog?"

Sue interjected promptly, "Clair, you're all dressed up for the picture, and you're not going out in the yard and have that dog jump on you."

That negative comment didn't deter Clair in the least. Her second question came without missing a beat. "Do you want to come upstairs and see my dolls?" Since the dolls weren't going to soil her perfectly pressed dress, there was no reason to debate this question. The answer was yes and I tried to catch up with Clair's energetic climb as she ascended like a Sherpa on Mount Everest. I was straggling ten steps behind.

Once more Sue rebutted, "Clair, he doesn't want to go up there and see your dolls, because what he will really see is all those boxes and other clutter and mess." I guess Sue was wrong about what I wanted, because we were already at the top step before she finished that sentence. Clair showed me to her room and introduced her assorted dolls, Barbies and teddy bears included. Since she couldn't hold them all while she looked for a hidden one, she offered one to me.

It was picture time and the handsome foursome posed on the couch. After I completed the task with wedding photographer proficiency, I then posed on the couch with Clair and Jaxon. Ed took our pictures. Jaxon sat on my lap and Ed commented, "I really don't know what your magnetism is with my kids, but I have a hard time getting Jaxon to sit on my lap and here he is climbing onto your lap on your first visit." I didn't claim to have a Pied Piper secret about our magical relationship, but it was a treat for me. If euphoria or exhilaration is better than joy, it was both of those things and more besides that I experienced at that photo shoot. I had a bounce in my step as I was off to Walgreen's to get the pictures developed. They were so clear and captured the Smith Family warmth so well that I voted myself the Yusuf Karsh portrait photographer award. Could his pictures of King or Kennedy, Marian Anderson or Picasso be ranked any higher than Ed and Sue, Clair and Jaxon? I was confident that I was in Karsh's award category even if I won by only one vote, my own.

I had to show them the pictures the next day. That presented another opening into their lives. I would occasionally drop in on the family when I was riding my bike and several times they invited me for dinner. I would read with the children, and I even began to offer another service that the fullest of full service churches did not offer. Since Jaxon was not religious but instead a particularly rambunctious two year old, I would take him to the playground on the corner when the rest of the family was attending Mass on Saturday evening. While Clair's initial appearance in church found her a place of prominence, Jaxon found a place on the slide, climber or the swings more appealing.

If that were not enough service from the church, I made one more offer that the family rejected initially, mulled over with some caution later and still later accepted with enthusiasm. I asked them if they would like me to babysit for their kids, so that Ed and Sue could go out on New Year's Eve. At first they doubted that I was serious and questioned that I wouldn't have better things to do on that night. Sue said, "I'm sure you really don't know what you're getting into, and you certainly have a better offer than to babysit on New Year's Eve."

However, once I convinced them that New Year's Eve was the consummate couple's night and that priests really don't fit in very well, they decided to take me up on the offer. I told them, "My sister, Mary Margaret, is eager to come and share the evening with me and would be happy to watch Clair and Jaxon." They relented and agreed that I might just as well spend the evening at their house with Mary Margaret. Otherwise, I was likely to be at Mary Margaret's house on New Year's Eve, the two of us alone together.

It was a brisk, crisp holiday evening when we got to the Smith's about 8:30 and helped Sue and Ed put the kids to bed. They brushed their teeth and we read them a story. Then we all prayed together. After the partiers left for the evening, Mary Margaret and I went to the living room to watch television. We had been shown the refrigerator that was full of beverages and the pantry with a variety of snacks. We were instructed to help ourselves. At about 10:15 in the middle of the news, Jaxon came creeping down the steps on his butt, one step at a time, holding on to the spindles supporting the banister. He was stealthy in his movements and very quiet on the deep carpet, but when he hit the bottom I noticed that there was a thud in the hall behind us. I went to pick him up and asked him, "Jaxon, how did you get here with the fence on the side of your crib up"? No answer, he seemed to be in a trance. I persisted, "Jaxon, you shouldn't be up. It's way past your bed time. Let's go back to bed."

He twisted and thrashed in my arms and was in charge at his house, "No."

"Jaxon, lets get a snack and then it is time to go back to bed."

Even louder the second time and with a stern voice, he shouted, "No" and made stubborn fists at his sides to emphasize his defiance.

He was rebellious, but I was tricky and confident that he could be bribed. We went to the kitchen and found the desired snack, a cookie and a small glass of milk. "Now it is time to go back to bed. Your mommy and daddy don't expect to find you up when they get home or I'll get fired. Finish up your last swallow of milk and let's go upstairs."

Jaxon was not impressed about my future unemployment and didn't really care much about his parent's expectations. He seemed to say, "Well, see if I care; they're at a party anyway." When he opened his mouth he announced, "No, I'm staying up." He ran out of the kitchen and down the hall. Mary Margaret was watching the crowd in The Big Apple.

He laid down on the couch in the living room next to me as the ball began to descend on Times Square. I could watch the ball descend, but I would not see Jaxon ascend to his second floor bedroom. As a babysitter, I had dropped the ball.

Clair was in the holiday spirit of a "long winter's nap" and had no concerns about the beginning of the New Year, but Jaxon was going to witness it in a semi-conscious trance. Mary Margaret and I watched the TV, availed ourselves of the goodies and exchanged good wishes for the New Year without banging any pots or exploding any fireworks. Jaxon was cozy in the crevice of the couch with a pillow under his stomach.

At 2:30 we heard the garage door open and Jaxon's parents entered by the kitchen door. He was the first one to greet them and jump into Ed's arms. Ed was somewhat bleary eyed from celebrating and a bit disappointed by Jaxon's Energizer Bunny presence. Sue was not surprised by Jaxon's presence in the kitchen and explained casually, "Oh Jaxon! Sometimes he walks in his sleep. I guess we should have told you this so you would have been warned about what to expect. One night he wandered outside and we found Jaxon asleep in the neighbor's car in the driveway between our houses. We're really glad you were here tonight because at least he stayed inside." She added the last comment with a wry smile.

My presence in the family was recognized by Ed in a flattering way some months later. He asked me to give a talk to the people on his sales team at the pharmaceutical company where he worked. It was good for my ego to address these top flight drug reps who exude confidence and pizazz. They seemed appreciative, and Ed confirmed the worth of my talk. "You are so honest and convincing when you preach. That's the quality that I want in all my people." I was reassured by this compliment from a drug rep, because sometimes I feared that my preaching was a non-narcotic sleep aid.

When Clair was in first grade, she invited me to come to her school for Grandparents' Day. Since her real grandparents were out of town, in Indiana and Louisiana, I got to be a proxy grandpa. I was proud, and somewhat self-conscious about playing grandpa, wondering what people might think about a priest in that role. However, nobody at Meramec School knew that I was a priest, because none of the "for real" grandparents were from our parish. All of the intimidation that I felt was of my own doing. The students sang a song and the class recited a poem. Most of the grandparents sat on the floor and we enjoyed some snacks. Each of the children brought a cupcake to their grandparents. I was beaming when Clair, my fairy granddaughter, brought me a cupcake with pink icing. It was the best cupcake that I ever ate. It helped me understand the comments of grandparents who prize that role more than parenting.

The New Year's Eve experience was the last time that I babysat for the Smith family. It wasn't because I bungled it too badly with Jaxon's performance, but because Ed's job moved them to Philadelphia before the New Year came around again. It was sad for me to see them leave, and I had my last time to play with the kids on the dining room floor when all the furniture was gone and the house was bare. We sat there and I told them a story. Then Clair pointed at the back of my arm and asked, "What's that"? She was curious about the droopy skin hanging down on the back of my elbows. She was too observant for my own good.

"Clair, did you ever pull on your shirt and stretch it until it sags? That's the way a man's skin gets when he is old enough to be your grandpa." I had to cover my embarrassment with a sheepish grin as I gave her a hug as tight as any grandpa should give. I hoped that they weren't planning a Great Grandparents' Day, but I definitely would have gone had I been invited.

My heart was heavy and I squinted away the tears waving good-bye as the Smith's drove off to Philadelphia. Ed handed me an envelope with a farewell gift card. It was made by Clair. I was entitled to receive one free plane trip to Philadelphia and a week's stay in the guest room at the Smith's new home. As the car disappeared around the corner, it was a bitter sweet moment; bitter about the sad loss and sweet with longing and expectation about the future visit. Fall colors filled the tree lined street as they disappeared, but I was like an anxious kid yearning to cash in this wonderful Christmas present.

I went to their home the following autumn when they were all settled in and the kids had returned to school. We hiked together in the dazzling foliage of the Valley Forge Park, kicked soccer in the backyard and had a picnic together. I had another chance to tuck Clair in at night. Clair had appeared out of the blue as a Sunday morning delight. She brought me into their family and I brought them into the family of a full service church with my photo session. Now at the Smith home, I was experiencing the most warmth that the City of Brotherly Love could offer. I had been renewed, because God let her face shine upon me (Ps. 80) in the Godly glow of Clair's twinkle.

Now she is a twenty-year-old coed at the University of Colorado. I will never forget that day in her youth when she entrusted her tiny hand to me in front of all those people. Now I give her a big hand for all of her accomplishments and the hope that she represents for a more beautiful and blessed world. I can only wonder who will be the next person she will touch and enliven by merely extending her hand and manifesting God's ordinary miracles.

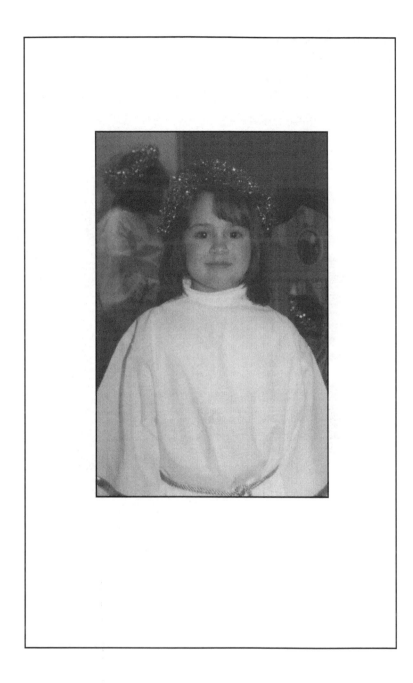

LAUREN BLUMENTHAL

The very act of storytelling, of arranging memory and invention according to
the structure of the narrative, is by definition holy.
Kerry Temple, *Notre Dame Magazine* – Autumn, 2011

I WAS NEW AT ST. JOSEPH PARISH, but the pleading and deep concern
was the same old story that priests hear in every parish. It is the cry of a
grandmother worried about her grandbaby who is not baptized. Add to
that the concern for their child who is married outside the church and
the situation becomes harder to address. Complicate the situation further
with the fear that the baby is dying, and any humble priest is tempted to
run away like Jonah who boarded a vessel heading away from Nineveh, the
city assigned him by God. I thought this was a situation only God could
address. I was fearful about intruding, and I certainly had no notion about
how to right all of the complexities and issues of this situation.

Mrs. Corteville's grandchild, Lauren, was afflicted with leukemia
of the worst kind. Lauren's parents, Jane, and her husband, David
Blumenthal, were both physicians at the prestigious Washington
University Medical Center. When I first came to know the family, Lauren
was one and a half years old. While I was more than a little apprehensive,
I mustered my courage and I visited their home during my first month at
St. Joseph's Parish. It was with considerable trepidation that I rang their
doorbell. Would I be welcomed or viewed as a meddler in an already trou-
bled situation? I presented myself as the neighborhood priest who had just
heard the sad news of Lauren's sickness, and I wanted to visit to see how
our parish community could assist them. My reception was so warm; I
knew that Mrs. Corteville must have told her daughter, Jane, that she had
called in God's reinforcements.

Jane and David were both slim and athletic in appearance with such warm and personal charm that they were the dream doctors that any patient hopes will be their doctor. Professionally, Jane served as a fetologist, diagnosing and treating abnormalities in unborn babies. David worked as a rheumatologist. Whatever might be their expertise when they wore their white coats with their names embroidered on the pocket, at home they were down-to-earth parents who had two other boys, Jordan and Colin, both older than Lauren. I was ushered into the family room immediately and saw a house that prized children's art as much as the Louvre treasured the Mona Lisa. It was everywhere, and maybe that helped explain the absence of a television.

I told them that I was new to the area and I asked them how long they had called this neighborhood home. I realized their self-effacing ease and total transparency when they said, "We haven't been here very long, just long enough to almost get arrested and have our kids removed by the DFS." They continued, "We were able to afford this lovely house in this great neighborhood because the elderly recluse who lived here let the house go to wreck and ruin. We got it for a song, but that meant that we would have to live through its total rehab. Once Jordan, our six-year-old was talking to someone at school and mentioned that he lived in the basement. He had a bruise and explained it by his accidental fall down the steps. The teacher knew that doctors living in this upscale neighborhood shouldn't be keeping their kids in the basement, so they reported us to the Child Abuse Hotline. They came to inspect the house and saw that it was impossible for us to do this total renovation and still live in the ordinary living area. They left without arresting us, but made several follow up visits to make sure that the work was actually progressing and our kids would not be relegated to a dungeon forever. David and I were really hoping that we as parents wouldn't be relegated to a dungeon for a life sentence either." It was clear that these two were about as unpretentious and comfortable as the sweatpants Jane was wearing.

I told them a bit of my previous assignments and some encounters that I had with burglars, police and shootings in my life. We all knew that we were survivors.

When I first met Lauren, she was tiny and pale. Her skin gave away her ill state of health. However, in all other respects she was a normal, active baby who wasn't lacking in attention from her family. Her big brothers were competitive with each other, but caring in their interactions with Lauren. They all knew how to keep busy and not suffer from boredom. It was clear that their children were the main focus for these parents as there was no television anywhere to be seen. My first visit was short and comfortable. All of the anxiety that I had felt in my walk over to their house had been misplaced. After this first brief encounter, I knew this energetic family would always welcome me. Before I left, I told them that I would be happy to organize a program at St. Joseph's to assist them in any way they would like. They told me that Samuel UCC down the street had already started a project on their behalf. I said we would work together with them and share in providing any assistance, childcare, grocery shopping, laundry, transportation, anything they needed that would help.

I began to visit on a regular basis and was always charmed by their homey warmth. Soon it was time for Lauren's second birthday. If I ever doubted my importance to the family, my doubts were allayed at party time. Jane called and invited me to the party and explained the exclusivity of this event. "We are only inviting my mom and you to the party. We want to do something to mark the occasion, but Lauren has a deeply compromised immune system. The more people and the more germs she is around, the greater likelihood that she will become even sicker. So if you don't have a cold and are feeling well, please come. It won't be much, but we will have a small party together." During that visit, we had some conversation about their house and neighborhood. Then it was revealed that their next-door neighbors were this delightful couple, Dr. Henry Lattinville and his wife, Marie. "If your family is not living close to relatives and their grandparents live in another state, there are no better people to be your kids' grandparents than Dr. Lattinville and his wife."

David professed the reason for his pride and confidence in being in such close proximity to these wonderful people. "When I was in medical school and going through the surgical rotation, there was a doctor in charge of neural-surgery at Washington U.'s Medical School. I don't want to mention his name but he was the rudest, most arrogant, cocky and overbearing person that I have ever met. When I was on the surgical rounds and went to observe his procedures, he was loud and abusive, shouting at the nurses and other attending physicians. In the heat of his anger, he would throw instruments around the operating theater and they would bounce off the walls. If an assistant handed him an instrument in the wrong way, it could start a third world war. This guy didn't just act like the fourth person of the Blessed Trinity, but he acted like the other three, whoever they were, ought to get in line behind him. I almost quit medical school by telling myself that I didn't want to be doctor if that was the way that I was going to turn out. But then I rethought it, considering that there are many good doctors, I wasn't predestined to become like this ogre.

"Then one day, I received an invitation to observe a particularly sophisticated brain operation that only a few students were invited to observe. This was cutting edge and I knew classmates who would have paid for the privilege of being there. At first, I was tempted to refuse the invitation, because I didn't want to be contaminated by this despicable individual, but then I reconsidered. I thought if I refuse to attend, this will be on my record and this decision might close doors for me in the future. I thought the better of it, and so I agreed to attend."

"The invitation stated that this in-charge physician would be ably assisted by a doctor named Henry Lattinville. I had never heard of him, of course, just being a medical student, but the invitation highlighted some of his very impressive credentials. He had been the president of the American Academy of Neural Surgeons. However, I had never heard of him and so in my mind a "no name" was not going to reform the Bozo whom I disliked. The day came for the surgery, and I found myself in the viewing area of this surgical suite. I really didn't know who Dr. Lattinville was, and I certainly couldn't tell anything with the gowns, hairnets, and face masks. All I could see was that this unknown man I presumed to be

Dr. Lattinville was a gentleman with bright, warm eyes. The procedure had hardly begun when the chief expressed himself in the boisterous and demeaning fashion that I feared would rule the day. He was at his worst, and I was once more questioning my decision about being there and wondering if this didn't undermine my personal dreams. The opening phrase of the Hippocratic Oath says, 'Above all, do no harm' and every time my nemesis spoke he harmed someone's ego and polluted the environment. After a few minutes of this tragedy unfolded, Dr. Lattinville spoke up. 'Doctor, I am happy that you invited me to be here, and I am happy to assist and consult in this delicate surgery. However, I have to tell you that I can only do my best work in a peaceful and harmonious atmosphere. If that isn't what I can expect here, then it would be well for me to leave'."

"That's all he said while he was looking directly at the chief." David said this with wide-eyed disbelief. Even though the incident had happened years ago, it seemed like yesterday. "And in that three sentences and half a minute, he changed the atmosphere of the room and the spirit of everyone there. I'll never forget that, because he never made any accusatory comments, but only stated what he needed in order to bring his best self to the tedious situation. He did it without any finger pointing, only with the threat of walking out, he transformed rancor into calmness. He brought harmony and healing to that hospital situation."

"And then we buy this house and find out that the Lattinvilles, these great people, are our neighbors. Whenever I think of it, I shake my head in wonderment. How could we have ever planned that? We couldn't in a million years. One of the reasons why I am a doctor today is that I was touched by Henry Lattinville's example that day at the operation that I almost didn't attend. What I feared would be awful turned out to be my best day in med school. And now he is our kid's grandparent across the fence. When he is raking leaves, he stops and asks my children if they want to come over and jump into the pile. When their ball goes into his yard he invites them over to get it and shows them his roses and explains how he prunes his bonsai trees. Now tell me, how lucky, how blessed can one family be?"

The party was fun. The presents were opened, cake and ice cream were consumed, and no significant germs were spread. Lauren had made it to her second birthday with many bumps in the road, but the real chuckholes were right around the corner. She made her share of trips to Children's Hospital and spent time in isolation there. Once I went to visit her and told Jane that she could be excused. "Go for a walk outside, get some fresh air or go get a snack." I was flattered that she took me up on the offer and trusted me with her sick child. I never was far from the buzzer in case I needed the assistance of a nurse. In the midst of the visit, Lauren stood up in her crib with all of the tubes and cords twisted and tangled around her. I told her to stand still so that I could pick her up and try to sort out the bird's nest of stuff. All the while I held her and tried to untangle, I probably made things worse and tightened the knots. However, Lauren seemed happy with the holding and maneuvering and persisted in pressing powder-puffy toys into my face. When I put her down, I relented and called the nurse for assistance. Possibly, I should have done that at the outset, but I trust when I finished with my contortions that we both felt more loved. After all my futile efforts, our lives had become more entangled and her feet and legs were still tangled.

When it became time for a bone marrow transplant, the decision was made to take Lauren to the U. of Minnesota Hospital in Minneapolis, the highest ranking hospital in the U.S. for this sort of procedure. Her mother accompanied her there and together they had a wonderful experience. Lauren set the record for a speedy recovery, and they were back home in a matter of weeks. For a brief period, Lauren was thriving; then she made her first visit back to Children's Hospital in St. Louis. Their immediate determination was that the transplant had failed. Lauren was back in the same shape as before, except now she was much weaker because of the surgery she had just undergone. Now she had an even more compromised immune system. Further treatment and many emergency procedures were undertaken, but to no avail. During this time, Jane and David were expecting a fourth child. That would add to their excitement if their life ever seemed boring.

During the months of our new friendship, it was clear to me that these were parents who were in love with life and delighted in the potential of each person. They mentioned that some of their doctor friends were amazed they could afford to have more children. While I never inquired about their response to their colleagues, they mentioned to me: "It all depends of your priorities. We couldn't afford more children if we drove a Mercedes-Benz like they do. But if you drive a used van and can deal with a few food spills and stains on the upholstery, then it is possible." David and Jane had an abundance of wisdom that some of their elders lacked. And as I observed them, they probably had more laughs than many of their colleagues also. Some of these came from their ability to laugh at themselves.

During these months of travel and health heartbreaks, many people from both St. Joseph's Church and Samuel Church were supporting the family in countless ways. Meals were prepared and others went shopping for the family. People would pick up the dirty laundry on the back porch, and later in the week, fresh laundry and linens and towels appeared without any indication about who did the good deed. They were folded and on hangers in the place where they had been found made sparkling as if by the magic wand of a Tinker Bell. Folks took the boys to their soccer games or took them to the swimming pool or movies and then for a Big Mac and fries. One of the difficulties in caring for a sick child is the lack of attention and concern for the healthy siblings. In all of these situations, I would hear the family rave about the support that they got from many people whom they didn't even know. They could hardly speak their gratitude enough. It was directed to the community, because particular individuals were usually unknown, unless they were people involved in direct childcare.

Sometimes I would get calls from parishioners wanting to know how they could help. One of the calls I received came from Penny Duke who was a doctor, too. She was not married, and as an anesthesiologist, worked regular hours in the operating room of St. John's Mercy Hospital. She was concerned that she never got called to help in any way. "I put my name on the list, and I never hear from anyone," she protested.

"I used to be on the swimming team, and so I would be as good at taking those boys to the pool as anyone. And besides that I'm a doctor, so you would think that I would be trusted and on the top of the call list." She would exhale in a huff trying to make the situation of being overlooked appear even more unbearable than she or I actually thought it was.

I said, "Maybe these people know more about you than we think they do, Penny." It was a great time to visit and tease. "All I can say, Penny, is that you signed up and since you never get called, you are the luckiest person of all. I don't handle any of those lists, so I can't tell you how the decisions are made or who gets called and when they get called. But I will tell you this much. If you sign up and you don't get called, you still get all the grace and blessing for your volunteering, even if you don't have to do any of the work. That's really a good deal," I said enthusiastically trying to placate a very good-hearted and deeply compassionate person who could not imagine enduring what her colleagues were suffering. She wanted to do her part to ease their pain.

Lauren continued to be hospitalized more often; sometimes it appeared that the treatments were mere experiments. People who are sick often suspect, rightly or wrongly, that is the case with teaching hospitals. One day the sad news was delivered to the family. "It's impossible for us to tell you this, but we can't do anything more for Lauren here at St. Louis Children's Hospital. We have tried everything that is possible for her treatment. It is time for you to take Lauren home." While they didn't actually say it, they meant, "Take her home to die." Death sentences are hard enough to hear, especially if the victim is your own loved one. But all parents have that genetic math marker inside their head and heart that tells them that their children are not supposed to die before they die. At this point, the love of life that surged through the very being of Jane and David had to have them question the need or reason to have children at all. However, the life-giving miracle that they had experienced so often won out and ruled the day for them once more.

Even some of their hospital colleagues at Washington University would say some strange things which weren't consoling. "I don't understand, here you are, both doctors, and you have a child who is incurable. How could this happen?" Jane was miffed by this type of illogic and said, "Where does that come from? I can't believe my own ears when I hear something like that. What does being a doctor have to do with whether or not your child is healthy?" Maybe it was the type of thinking that helped to assure these doctors that their own child could not get deathly ill. As they say, "Denial is more than a river in Egypt."

When Jane had returned home from the transplant surgery at the University of Minnesota, she spoke about the survivor's guilt that she had experienced with Lauren having such a remarkable recovery and other children dying even as they awaited a donor or a match for their procedure. "It was hard to see those parents, and I was so clumsy in trying to express my sympathy for their immeasurable loss. It was so terrible that I didn't even want to think about it." Now she seemed to be heading in that very direction and words could not capture her numb disbelief. She had experienced birth and was like every mother believing that she was totally unique and had just experienced the eighth wonder of the world. Now she felt like she was on the track for an inevitable train-wreck. She could see the light coming at her down the tunnel. We visited and prayed while Lauren was home and very weak.

David and Jane experienced another ray of hope for Lauren's healing. Jane knew a pediatric oncologist named, Dr. Donna Wall. She had taken care of Donna during one of her complicated pregnancies. Dr. Wall was at the hospital affiliated with St. Louis University Medical School, Cardinal Glennon Memorial Hospital. Somehow they got word that Donna had some cutting edge notions about treating Lauren's disease. David and Jane had their medical insurance with a group at Washington U. They crossed their fingers and asked an important question. They were cautious and hopeful, even as they feared that the answer would be a crushing negative. "Could we use the group medical insurance that we have with Washington U. Medical Center at a Catholic Children's Hospital across town?"

"You can pick one doctor there and we will honor her bills," they were told. They were more shocked than merely surprised. When they had posed this question they feared that they were wasting their breath. In an instant, their overwhelming anxiety both about Lauren and the cost issue was replaced by such a quick and easy positive answer. God is very good indeed. It was their first miracle in Lauren's healing. Unbelievably, Washington University Medical Center insurance would pay the bill at the Catholic children's hospital.

Doctor Wall studied Lauren's case. She had an idea about a cocktail of several experimental drugs that had shown some promise. Lauren was admitted and received the drugs. However, she showed no response. She only became weaker. In the meantime, David and Jane were exploring more options. Joan, a co-worker of Jane's, was spending some time at a friend's summer house. He was a hematologist at Washington University who mainly treated another type of blood disease called sickle cell disease. One morning he was opening his mail and showed Jane's co-worker a manuscript he was sent to review. "Why did they even send this to me?" he said. "This is not even in my area of expertise." Joan looked at the manuscript. It described a new drug to treat the rare form of Leukemia that afflicted Lauren. The drug showed an 80% response rate in individuals who had failed all other treatments. Joan asked him if he would leak the paper. He said that was against the pledge he took as a reviewer that he would not leak content prior to publication. However, he knew David and Jane and wanted to help. The next day he called David and gave him the manuscript.

To David and Jane it looked too good to be true. The drug was Chi Ling, a Chinese herbal medication. The active ingredient was Arsenic Trioxide. It sounded toxic. But the paper indicated there was little toxicity. They wondered if they could trust the source. Was the data fabricated? The only way to find out was to contact the lead author on the manuscript. The lead author was in Harbin China.

David, at the time, was working in a research laboratory with a doctor from China. She offered to contact the Chinese doctor and get information. Everyday Lauren was becoming worse. She now was so weak she rarely walked. That evening, David, Jane and Xu Lin contacted the Chinese doctor. He wanted them to bring Lauren to China. That was out of the question; she was too weak. Xu Lin convinced the doctor to smuggle the medication to her in an unmarked box. It would be very unlikely to be detected by a postal inspector.

Meanwhile, the parents approached Dr. Wall and asked if she would give the Chinese medicine. She went before in institutional review board (IRB) and asked for special dispensation to give a drug without a name, that had never been used in the USA and with no safety profile. The board said no. "This could be bee spit" was their response. A week later the drug arrived. It was put in the closet since it could not be used.

Dr. Wall was doing research on her own. She identified a drug from Switzerland which showed some promise. She contacted the drug company who said they would be happy to admit Lauren to the trials, but she would need to come to Switzerland.

On Good Friday, Lauren became gravely ill. She had a serious infection and no immune fighting cells. Her bone marrow had been re-placed by the Leukemia. She was admitted to the Intensive care unit. Dr. Wall contacted the drug company. They agreed to send a courier on the next flight to New York. However, she would have to meet the courier at the plane in person since the FDA did not approve these drugs. This technically was illegal. On the day Dr. Wall was to meet the courier, Dr. Penny Judge was leaving St. John's Mercy hospital where she worked as an anesthesiologist. As she was heading for her car, she encountered Dr. Wall's husband, Alex Mills, MD, who worked as an anesthesiologist in the hospital emergency room. They greeted each other on the path, but Penny sensed a somber tenseness about Dr Mill's demeanor. "Are you all right?" she inquired as they stopped for a momentary visit. "You look wor-ried. Are you feeling okay?"

"Well, I'm really in a Catch 22 and I don't know what to do. I'm supposed to work until midnight. At the same time, my wife has to go to New York to get some drugs for the treatment of a very sick child. I told her that I would be home to babysit and put the kids to bed, but I really don't know how I'm going to do that. I never found anyone to trade with and take part of this shift. So as you can see, I am really in a bind."

"Problem solved," Penny said with her usual buoyant confidence. "Here's your answer. I'll go home, eat and get some rest. I'll be back at the hospital in plenty of time to cover for you. You go home to be Doctor Mom to your kids tonight. Then Donna can get to the airport, get the drugs and start the healing process for that sick child." Penny had no idea who the sick child was. Unbeknownst to Penny, she was performing the service for Lauren's family that she had always longed to offer. And in the big picture, God's plan, she was doing what only she could do. Other people could do laundry and take Lauren's brothers to the pool, but nobody else on the volunteer list was an anesthesiologist. God's providence was at work, clear and simple.

Dr. Donna Wall's family was being cared for and a new chapter was about to begin in the treatment of Lauren's leukemia. Dr. Wall procured the precious bundle of pharmaceuticals, returned to St. Louis, and rushed to Cardinal Glennon Hospital to inspect the contents and mix the chemicals she hoped would be the magic elixir that would heal Lauren's killer disease. She began the infusion of the Swiss drug. But after two days there was little response. Lauren was dying. She brought David and Jane into a conference room and told them Lauren would die. Then she surprised them by asking, "What happened to that Chinese medicine?" She asked the family to bring it in. She said she had no hope it would work, but she would give the medicine herself and tell the nurse to look the other way since what she was doing was illegal and forbidden by the hospital IRB. She promised to take the heat if anyone found out. She administered the Chinese drug along with the Swiss drug. After two weeks, the Leukemia was in remission. In fact, there was no trace of the Leukemia in Lauren's body even though the most sensitive genetic tests had been used.

The news of this miraculous cure spread through the medical community like wildfire. Doctors at other hospitals started experimenting with both drugs. In the end, they found that the exact sequence and duration of dosing that Lauren received was the most effective.

When she was assured that the Leukemia cells had disappeared and was confident that the next step in the process, that Lauren was growing her own healthy cells, could occur, she called Lauren's family, and came to visit them at home. She dragged herself up the steps and into the house. Dr Wall fell into a chair verging on exhaustion. The pressure valve on her overtaxed emotions was about to explode. There was the constant anxiety of Lauren's delicate health, the traveling to assure the procurement of the medicine continents away, and finally the use of unproven and unapproved substances for treatment of this beleaguered toddler.

"David and Jane, here's the situation," she blurted out knowing that every second counted. "I got the drugs that we spoke about and we may have set a record for their procurement. At least they are here and Lauren is still with us. I can't believe that any insurance company is going to pay for something that is considered such an experiment, but we know that there is nothing else hopeful on the horizon. So, I have the drugs to give to you along with the directions about how they are to be administered. You're doctors and you can do this here at your house, and then I will have Lauren come into the hospital every week or ten days for tests and examination. The insurance will pay for that, and we can plan and evaluate as we go along. You can keep all the proper records about the treatment just as if we were doing this in the hospital so that we can make adjustments as necessary. And of course, stay in touch daily and call me with any questions or concerns that you might have." It was a conversation followed by all the details necessary to begin the treatment. Dr. Wall had to be the good fairy or an angel sent by God, because she kept hope alive in their hearts.

As the first weeks passed and Lauren was still alive, there were real concerns about whether she was improving or getting worse. Some of the doctors on the team thought that she had to get worse before she could get better. Whenever there was a consideration like this, all David and Jane had to remember was that no one at Children's Hospital held out any hope for healing. There wasn't any "getting better" in their vocabulary. However slow, tedious, and uncertain the evaluative process was, after several months, it was clear that Lauren was getting better. In her weakest state, her bone marrow had been completely replaced by leukemic cells and there were no signs of normal cells from the bone marrow donor. Yet slowly but surely, the donor marrow repopulated the empty marrow left by the Leukemia. The doctors were astounded.

This was the gateway to the third miracle. The experimental drugs that had been brought into the country for Lauren's treatment were later approved by the Food and Drug Administration for Lauren's type of leukemia that was eighty percent fatal. It became eighty percent curable when patients were treated in the same way that Lauren had been treated by her parents in her family home.

Jane was once plagued with survivor's guilt when Lauren left the U. of Minnesota Hospital so very healthy after her bone marrow transplant. Now she was beginning to get another case of the same guilt. "How could this blessing be lavished on us?"

I told her, "Jane, this is God's great plan that this disease has become so very curable through your love and diligence and medical competence. You and David had to be the people who could treat your own daughter and keep such accurate records that the medical establishment could replicate your efforts with other children."

Lauren's third birthday was approaching, and Jane wanted to celebrate by inviting all of those people who had supported the family in the many ways that I mentioned. Some people had done the heavy lifting and many more had done the behind the scenes things like pray for a miracle or two or three. She planned a big party at the community center in the park and spent much of the early Sunday afternoon with friends decorating for the gala. There were streamers and balloons everywhere and games for all the children and cake and ice cream and punch. The party was to begin at two in the afternoon, and David was bringing Lauren and her three brothers over to the park. As they drove along David said to Lauren, "Isn't it wonderful that all of these people are coming to party with you to celebrate your birthday?"

Lauren responded with a knowledge way beyond her innocent years, "They're not coming for my birthday. They're really coming to see me, because they didn't think that I'd live this long."

In reporting this conversation to me David said, "When your three-year-old daughter says this to you there is only one thing to do. Turn up the radio and keep driving."

Shortly after Lauren's healing, Jane and David lost their health insurance at Washington University Hospital because they hit the spending cap. While this was shocking and horrible, it didn't rank nearly as high on the horror scale as almost losing a child. Fortunately, they were able to get jobs at the Cleveland Clinic, which covered the health insurance and brought them much closer to Grandma Corteville in Detroit. She needed a doctor daughter closer to her than St. Louis. That also made it easier to care for the grandchildren she loved so much.

For a few years, Jane, David and the kids would return to visit with their St. Louis friends. Lauren's top priority, however, was not the zoo or the City Museum, but to visit Dr. Wall at Cardinal Glennon Hospital. Lauren had a favorite Barbie doll that she called her Donna Wall doll. She gave it to Dr. Wall as a thank you gift. Jane said that Lauren's gift brought a laugh to everyone at Cardinal Glennon Hospital who all agreed that Dr. Donna Wall was the "least Barbiesque woman you would ever meet." Dr. Wall proudly displayed the doll in her office and was eager to tell Lauren's story. Lauren certainly had her own evaluative criteria, but her opinion probably had as strong a foundation as any recognition that Dr. Wall could receive from the American Medical Association.

Lauren is now 18 years old and a student at Kent State University. After her harrowing medical course, it is not surprising that she has some medical problems. However, she is a happy, giving person who shows God's love shines brightly. She is majoring in fashion design. She wants to design fashionable clothes for people with special needs, as she once was.

Immaculate Conception Parish

JUST WHEN I THOUGHT that I had overcome my xenophobia I was assigned to Immaculate Conception Parish in a booming, sprawling farming area that was getting developed quicker than the birds could move out of the trees that were felled by the bulldozers. If the birds were homeless, residences for new arrivals were sprouting up faster than dandelions in April. There I realized my fear and anger toward folks who flee the city to find paradise away from crime and race issues. There was no pepper in the salt of sleepy hollow called Dardeene Prairie, MO.

During my two-year stay there, I was shocked to celebrate more children's funerals than I ever had in my previous thirty-five years of parish ministry. I raised questions about some environmental contamination that dated back to the Manhattan Project and necessitated a Super Fund Cleanup Project in Weldon Springs at the edge of the parish boundaries. The publicity I generated made many people unhappy, because they had moved to the area thinking that they had discovered the Garden of Eden. The radioactive environment and infant deaths were the front page cover story in both the *Riverfront Times* and *Family Circle*. Some people, especially home builders and politicians, petitioned the Archbishop to move me.

Even as I celebrated numerous infant funerals, this situation became an eye-opener for the people who joined in my investigation and didn't simply dismiss me as a neurotic alarmist. A documentary movie regarding the history of the nuclear industry in the area has been released. It is entitled, *The Safe Side of the Fence*. I also witnessed some miracles of healing there and discovered that a major miracle was my own innerhealing and growing conviction that blanket condemnations of groups of people are stupid and unchristian.

"BE SHEPHERDS LIVING WITH THE SMELL OF THE SHEEP"

Pope Francis said, "Among the vulnerable for whom the Church wishes to care with particular love and concern are unborn children, the most defenseless and innocent among us. Nowadays efforts are made to deny them their human dignity and to do with them whatever one pleases, taking their lives and passing laws preventing anyone from standing in the way of this.

Yet this defense of unborn life is closely linked to the defense of each and every other human right. It involves the conviction that a human being is always sacred and inviolable, in any situation and at every stage of development." Ibid. *Evangelii Gaudium.* p. 153.

In *Family Circle* Jeannette Batz Cooperman, Ph.D said:
"Moving like sleepwalkers, the parents follow the small casket down the aisle and out the doors of Immaculate Conception Catholic Church of Dardenne Prairie, Missouri. They motion to Father Gerry Kleba to go to the cemetery without them; they have to get back to the hospital, where their other newborn struggles to breathe in her ICU tent. Father Kleba nods, but wonders how these parents can grieve the loss of their baby girl while hovering, sick with worry, over her twin.

On this particular Saturday, Father Kleba softly enters a hospital room, bends his 6'5" frame and folds a mother into his arms. She and her husband thought their little boy had a mild, survivable form of leukemia; they hadn't braced themselves for him to die.

As he tries to console her, he is flooded with images of other parishioners who have experienced this kind of pain, including this family's next-door neighbors, who lost an infant nine months earlier. He thinks too, about Ann Bachman. At least 10 babies have died since hers, and her singing has accompanied many of their funerals. But Ann's grief has also led her to research the links between cancers, brain diseases and the toxins that once polluted this area.

In the spring of 2000 Father Kleba came here as senior associate pastor. What he found shocked him, "This parish has more sick and dying children than I have ever experienced in my thirty-five years as a priest," he told the church's social-concerns committee.

Everybody felt there was more cancer here—and more miscarriages, birth defects, neurological problems. They spoke of how, before the government's nearly $1 billion cleanup began in the 1980s, kids used to joke that they'd glow if they drank from the water fountains at Francis Howell High School, a quarter mile north of the uranium processing plant.

Ann Bachman has shared with Father Kleba the photo of her newborn twins: David wears a baby bonnet that hides the missing top of his head....When Ann researched anencephaly on the Internet, she found several moms who suspected thorium as a cause. She joined a support group, the Center for Loss in Multiple Birth. Months later the president of the group called. They were curious as to how long her street was. The group had three members on that street, all of whom had lost babies.

Her street, Ann said, is only five blocks long.

In the fall of 2002 the Department of Energy finished its cleanup and departed. The social-concerns committee regrouped, too, to start a new direction. With Father Kleba assigned to another parish as of July 2003, nothing further has been done.

As for Father Kleba, he says, "You try to open other people's eyes. The home builders certainly didn't want anybody to think anything was askew. I just wish the only place in the country contaminated like that was Weldon Spring. These places aren't going away for 24,000 years. They can impact our children's grandchildren's grandchildren."

Uncommon Courage
March 9, 2004. pp. 69 – 77.

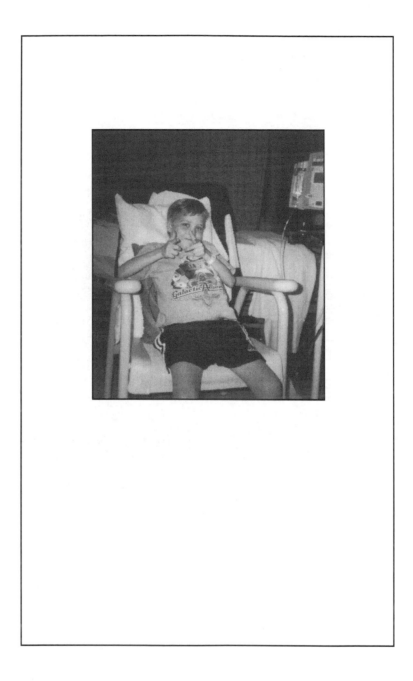

JUSTIN JACOB

"To Infinity and Beyond."

Buzz Lightyear – *Toy Story 2*

I DON'T REMEMBER EVER MEETING the Jacob family before I made that difficult trip to St. Louis Children's Hospital. I was new at Immaculate Conception Parish in Dardenne Prairie, MO, and I was overwhelmed by the size of this parish that was growing at the rate of one new family a day. Since I had spent most of my priesthood in small inner-city African-American parishes, and since most blacks in St. Louis are not Catholic, I was astounded by the size of the parish and had seldom been in a church that was so white. There was not one family of color. "No pepper in the salt," was the frequent thought that remained with me since my inner-city days. But the people there were very welcoming and the priests that I lived with were congenial. We were usually on the same page in terms of our personal theology and pastoral practice. Where there were differences, they were somewhat marginal and not the ones that caused any real friction. All that being said, the simple fact is that I barely had my feet on the ground at ICD. It was huge, with countless organizations and sports activities and thirteen Masses on a weekend. I tried to stay focused midst this whirl wind of activity.

There was always a list on the billboard with the names of parishioners who were in the hospital, and whenever one of the priests was going to St. Louis, he made an effort to visit them. If the sick person was a child in one of the children's hospitals in the city, we all tended to be doubly diligent. So it was that I got the opportunity to visit Justin Jacob, a first-grader who was in the hospital. He went to a neighborhood public school, which made it less likely that I would know him. The truth be told, there were so many people in the parish that I didn't know more than a few of the students in the parish school, which was right outside our back door. I was a spectator with all of life going on around me. I went to the hospital and found a youngster with beautiful sandy blond hair and very delicate features. He was a boy that I could easily describe as beautiful, except that seemed like the wrong adjective for a boy. As best I could understand on this first visit, he was the fourth of four boys in the family of Karen and Kevin. Karen worked in some capacity at a Kmart and Kevin worked as a chef and manager for Russo's Gourmet Catering, an upscale catering company. I visited for only ten minutes. I barely had time to introduce myself and get acquainted when Justin said, "You can leave now." I was taken aback, but thought this was the prevailing opinion when his parents didn't say that he shouldn't talk to Father that way. So I left somewhat miffed by the fact that I had spent so much time and effort in a corporal work of mercy and been dismissed so easily by a six-year-old.

I thought, "I'm big and dressed in a black suit, doesn't he know how important I am?" But I had the good sense to leave anyway.

As I drove home, I examined my conscience about whether I had ever been so casually dismissed, not to even consider the youthfulness of the patient who had shown me the door. When I got back home, I mentioned this brusque goodbye to some others on the staff, all of whom were aware of the sick boy's situation more than I was. I knew that they would understand how rude it was to give me the "bum's rush." Instead, rather than folks commiserating with me and sympathizing in my pity party, I got a totally different message. I heard people say, "You have to admire parents of sick kids who were able to instill this type of confidence in their children and encourage them to speak for themselves and keep some safe space around them." At first I couldn't believe what I was hearing. There certainly was a lot of wisdom in that kind of thinking, knowing that all patients have very little private space and are open to constant intrusions on their personhood.

Their comment was eye-opening for me. I didn't really know the history of Justin's illness, but he was both courteous and clear in making his statement that he was finished with me taking up his time and space. In retrospect, I was also happy that I mentioned this affront to Cathy, a staff member who was a mother herself, who gave me the insight. If I had not, I might have taken it as personal and left Justin's needs to be addressed by one of the other priests. Had I done that, I would have missed out on one of the life's bigger blessings.

It was clear to me that Justin was a very sick child, and I began to tell his story at many of the Masses that I celebrated. I also went to many of the grade school classes to solicit prayers and to get the students to design and color get well cards for Justin. It was a ministry to the sick that lots of the youngsters and their teachers enjoyed performing, and soon I found a bundle of cards packaged and tucked between the screen and the door at the entrance to the rectory. As time allowed, I took them over to Justin's house. In the beginning, I was quite casual about fitting this into my schedule, but I found that children would question me about their cards the very next day after I received them. If I hadn't taken them over to Justin's bedside, I looked heartless in the eyes of these diligent and caring artists. So visiting Justin with the cards became a priority. Since he was small and the printing was youthful and the spelling creative, either his parents or I would have to read them with him. His dad went to work early and came home in the middle of the afternoon. Frequently, he was the person sitting next to Justin's bed, which was in the family room of the house. It was my job to unwrap the cards and present them to the reader front side up. This was always an exciting time for Justin, but at times he could be a brutal art critic. "Look how sloppy that is," he might announce with disdain.

Kevin would always speak up for the artist and the care that had prompted the children to invest themselves in the project to begin with. "I'm not so sure that you could do all that much better, or not every-body is a great artist, but at least all of these children care," he would say in their defense. And if the critique was particularly cutting, he would threaten to stop reading them and put them aside until Justin thought he could behave better. That generally made Justin less harsh and outspoken, because he certainly enjoyed seeing all the colors and the designs and figuring out the motifs, which usually included stars, the sun, rainbows, flowers, and religious symbols like crosses and halos and churches with steeples. Sometimes the children sent some candy and other gifts to accompany their cards. A real bonding took place between Kevin and Justin as I opened the cards on one side of the bed and passed them behind the headboard to Kevin who held them and read them on the other side. Then we would put them on the covers and rejoice in the growing pile of art, color and energetic, youthful love that all the cards represented. The ones that slid off the pile and ended on the floor had to be retrieved immediately and treated with the respect accorded a museum piece.

When the word gets around the health care community of St. Louis about a particularly sick child, it seems to take very little time to get on the Make a Wish Foundation list. How this happens has never been clear to me, but in Justin's case, it was apparent that he wanted little in the way of attention from this fine organization. Most of his desires seemed to revolve around sports as his brothers were quite athletic and on several select teams in both hockey and soccer. There was a hockey stick signed by the whole St. Louis Blues team that had a place of importance on the mantle above the fireplace. I had also heard him speak about some desired memorabilia from the St. Louis Rams.

I knew a few people at the St. Louis Rams through my participation in a program called Leadership St. Louis, and I also knew that their quarterback at the time, Trent Green, had gone to Vianney High School. My cousin, Larry Furrer, had taught there for many years and was currently the principal. I stopped by the Rams' office one day unannounced and I was told that they were in a closed practice. I would not have access to any of the players. I had a chat with Adrian, my front office friend, and after a few minutes, the team came into the office building for lunch. She found Trent and cajoled him into visiting with me. I told him about my cousin, Larry, and he had only fond memories of his high school years and Larry's investment in the school and contact with the students. Then I told him Justin's story and his desire to have a football and a jersey and other Rams' goodies. He was delighted that I asked, "Father,

I'm thrilled to help sick kids in any way I can. I have some children, and so far, all of mine are healthy and I don't have to spend any time at the hospital with them. So if my visit and my gifts brighten up the days of one of these kids who see me as a hero, hey what better thing do I have to do but to make that child happy? I will get over to Justin's house next week since it's really close to Rams' Park.

I felt proud of myself for all the influence that I had in the world of big time professional sports, and I was thrilled to meet a star, but I was greatly impressed with Trent's attitude as the product of a Catholic school and a student of my cousin. The next time I was at Justin's house, they told me about the wonderful visit they had from Trent Green. I had helped to build a little bridge and brought a bit more joy into Justin's life. And without trying to be too smug and self-important, I did rejoice in being so influential in the world of NFL players.

It was clear that the people at the Make a Wish Foundation felt un-needed or under-appreciated by Justin's small wish list. Here was a child who was grateful for a hockey stick and a football while others wanted a trip to Disney World or a Sherpa ride to the top of Mount Everest. Make a Wish called and tried to convince Kevin and Karen that there was a lottery to be won by their sick child if he was more grasping and greedy and they shook their corporate head at the simplicity of his requests. They were miffed by Justin's casual acceptance, but finally Justin asked for something signif-icant and extraordinary. He wanted a computer hookup to his classroom that would allow him to tune in first grade at Twin Chimneys Elementary School. With the activation of a bed side computer, he could plug into class. Each time he spoke up, his picture appeared on a classroom white board. This made it possible for him to converse with the class, ask a question or participate in a discussion. While this was less exotic than some of the other requests that the Make a Wish Foundation received, at least there was some expense and sophistication involved in the gift. I asked Karen, "How often does Justin tune in to his first grade class?"

"Oh, he's just like his brothers," she replied, "he tunes in to school about half the time." His brothers were full-time students and she was a proud mother who was also quite a tease.

Sports were popular and get-well cards were cherished, but the one all time favorite pastime on Justin's list was watching the movie, *Toy Story 2*. Tim Allen played Buzz Lightyear, and Justin's favorite line from the movie was, "To Infinity and Beyond."

One early morning, Tim Allen, who had been told of Justin's love for Buzz Lightyear by the Make a Wish Foundation, called to talk to Justin. Karen told him that Justin was asleep, but that she would get him up. Tim was strong in his refusal, "I don't call sick children to disturb their day and to take the kids away from their much needed rest. Just tell me when you think that it will be a good time to call back and I will try again. If that isn't a good time, we'll try again and the third time will probably be the charm." Karen made a suggestion and Tim hung up to try later.

When the phone rang at the suggested time, Karen answered and said, "Someone is on the phone and he says that he is Buzz Lightyear. He would like to talk to you."

"Mom, I hate to tell you, but Buzz Lightyear isn't real, he's just a toy."

"Well, this person would like to talk to you, so why don't you take the phone and talk to him anyway and see who it is?" Karen suggested as she handed him the receiver.

Justin took it with a bit of skepticism, but after a few minutes, he was into a conversation with the voice on the other end. His eyes sparkled and the energy flowed. His voice became more dynamic, sometimes whispering and shouting at other times. There was an electric connection with the caller and Justin would scream, "To infinity and beyond." The conversation lasted for forty-five minutes, and he never again said that Buzz was merely a toy. Across the family room in the kitchen, there was a sparkle in Karen's eyes also, and it was highlighted by the moist, glassy quality that had Karen dabbing them with the dish towel in her hand. There was a giddy, joyful dance that accompanied her kitchen tasks.

Halloween was fast approaching, and there was a fire in the fireplace under the mantle where the prized sports treasures were on display. The crisp air and the crackling leaves painted with gaudy colors gave a special accuracy to the name of their subdivision, Canvas Cove. Spooks and spiders began to decorate the lawns in the area, and Halloween was at hand. I prompted the kids in the parish to remind them of the need for additional cards for Justin. The Halloween cards gave the children a chance to expand their artistic renderings beyond the religious sphere. Many of them came with a sampling of the Trick or Treat jokes that the artists were preparing to take door to door for their night time excursion.

One of the cards had this joke printed on its cardboard jack-o-lantern cut out. "What do ghosts have in their noses? BOOgers." Like all boys who are intrigued with bodily functions, this was one of Justin's favorites.

When I called the family on the eve of Halloween, they told me that Justin wasn't up to visitors, and he didn't want me to come. I had prepared myself for this rejection several months earlier, so I was accepting of this answer. On All Saints' Day, I was intending to visit Justin after the evening Mass. I returned to the rectory to find the light flashing on the base of the phone indicating that there was a message awaiting me on voice mail. The message told me to come as soon as I could after Mass. Justin had died during the All Saints' Day Mass at about the very time that I was remembering him from the altar. All Saints' Day was a perfect time to die, but that didn't diminish the heartbreak and grief.

I went to the house and the grandparents were already there. The family was awaiting the arrival of many more relatives. I lost track of time as I simply sat by the side of Justin's bed and pondered his lifeless body. I looked at Justin's beautiful face that was so very radiant and at peace. It was boyish and angelic. He had the most delicate eye-lashes that were so graciously curved and perfectly blond. I sat there silently. I visited and met dozens of relatives. I prayed with stricken grandparents, numbed with hollow and dark sadness and unable to speak. I would return to sit again and look at this innocent beauty so serene. I hugged Karen and Kevin and

163

looked for the brothers, who were hiding in their rooms or outside visiting with some of their friends and neighbors. I never thought that this beautiful life would end so soon. Looking back, I don't think that I ever realized how sick Justin was although I'm sure that in our many hours of visiting, his prognosis had been discussed. Longer lines of relatives streamed into the house and there was a general tenor of joy about life and comfort in the hugging that prevailed. And of course, there was food. I don't remember many tears, but I certainly remember my own inner conflict, a heavy brokenhearted shock that a young life had ended and a sense of peace. And then there was always the pleasantness of Justin's seraphic demeanor. He was such a beautiful, flawless child with soft, glowing skin and eyes; but he was so very sick. It was incomprehensible. Once all the family was there, we prayed together and Justin was taken from his home. His little body was carried out; his big spirit had been drifting away even as his cousins were arriving. Ecclesiastes reminds us, "There is a time to be born and a time to die."

I went to the funeral home on a Sunday afternoon and the crowd was enormous. Kevin took me aside, "Father, is it alright if all of Justin's first grade class come to the funeral Mass?"

In retrospect, I guess it was the most ordinary question in the whole world, and of course anybody who wants to come to a funeral is welcome, but I was shocked and wanted to respond abruptly: "What are you thinking, I don't want all those little kids in church for this sad moment, and besides that, don't you think that I will have a hard enough time preaching at this event without having to tailor-make my talk for seven year olds?" That's what I wanted to say. Oh, I almost forgot to mention that I would begin by saying, "Are you crazy supposing those little munchkins are welcome?" However, the Holy Spirit was working overtime; my better angel prevailed. "Kevin, whatever you think is best is what we want to do. Of course, the first graders are welcome. I will have our school principal contact the first grade teacher, Mrs. Miller, at Twin Chimneys School and make plans for some little ritual that will involve Justin's classmates."

I scooted out of the funeral home as quickly as I could thinking that I had more work to do on my homily than I imagined when I walked in. I wondered why I hadn't anticipated that question, but the fact is that I had not. I felt like I had been bushwhacked. I had to ponder and pray and then pray some more. As I did, a new sense of gratitude came over me realizing that I was in a much better position with this heads-up than I would have been if the first graders would have been getting off the school bus and I had no premonition about their front row attendance. As I prayed, I realized that it would have been a shame to allow Justin's passing to go unnoticed by the administration and his classmates at the public school. This was especially the case since the Make a Wish Foundation had made Justin electronically visible even when his first day of first grade was actually his last day in the classroom.

I had a sleepless night and the Monday morning of the funeral arrived with dark, bleak weather. A cold rain was pelting down and driving the leaves that clung to the branches into winter submission. The kids arrived in church like wet puppies. One other unfulfilled Make a Wish was to be fulfilled on this morning. Justin had longed for a ride on a fire truck. As the church bell tolled, the chartreuse fire truck rolled up in the place usually reserved for a black hearse. Even though the sky was leaden gray, the rain made the yellow-green truck shiny bright and the yellow slickers of the firemen even brighter. Setting on the top of the truck was Justin's little casket, and the strong nimble firefighters were as delicate with this precious cargo as a jeweler with the Hope Diamond. While the thunder rumbled after a lightening flash, these giants of men carried Justin into church. The rain was rushing off the back of their fire hats just as they were designed to disgorge water at a five alarm fire. The first graders had taken their places standing by the pews as an honor guard down the center aisle of Immaculate Conception Church. In its 140 years, the parish had seen final celebrations for prominent members and holy pastors, but no celebration had greater solemnity and tears. There weren't many dry eyes and the weather had little to do with it. Mine were as moist as the firemen's and I hadn't been outside.

All through the previous sleepless night, I thought about what theme could touch the children at this teachable moment. I knew the mystery of undeserved suffering was not something that anyone could comprehend, but if I could communicate with the children, then it was likely I would touch the hearts of the adults and especially the broken hearts of the Jacob family. It was homily time, and I had taken my globe for a show and tell. I asked the children sitting in the three front pews of this standing room only gathering of 350 people, "What is this I'm holding in my hand?"

"It's a globe," some said while others said, "Planet earth."

"How many of you children think that the earth is flat or do some of you think that the earth is round?"

I got the resounding answer that I expected. "It's round," they all shouted as if to scoff at any members of the Flat Earth Society who may be in attendance.

Then I held the globe higher and spun it as fast as I could. "Do you think that the earth spins, or does the earth stand still?"

"The earth spins," they all agreed with considerable confidence.

I warned them now that the questions were about to get trickier and that maybe I would call on someone who raised his or her hand. "I won't call on anyone who shouts out an answer," I warned. Now think about this. "Besides being round and spinning at a dizzying speed of thousands of miles an hour, does the earth fly through the air or just hang in the sky like a dazzling Christmas tree ornament? Now think about this. Who knows the answer?"

A cautious little girl raised her hand with tentative confidence. I pointed to her. "Yes, let's hear the answer from the girl in the bright orange dress," I said hoping that her answer would be right because I didn't want any first grader to feel like a loser on this day of such loss. I said, "Stand up and speak up so that everyone can learn something here. Does the earth just hang in the sky or fly through the air?"

My selected redhead in the orange dress stood up and surprised me with her confidence. "The earth flies through the air," she announced.

"Very good, now let me ask you another question. What does the earth fly around"? Since she had a quizzical look of uncertainty, I chose another eager student to answer. This time I called on a boy. "Yes, young man with the yellow tie, can you tell me what the earth flies around?"

He was quieter, but taller and even turned to the rest of the church rather than talk directly to me. So with Jeopardy game show winner confidence, beginning with a question he said, "What does the earth fly around? It flies around the sun."

So now it was my time to review, "We all agree, the earth is round. The earth spins. The earth flies. Do we all think that is the way this planet acts?" As I spoke I stood before the children and took my twelve inch globe of the blue planet on a practice spin and orbit with my other hand being the sun. As I completed this bit of astronomy, I scratched my head and asked, "How many of us thought that we were walking at home or at school or at church today on a flat planet that was perfectly still? Did we get out of breath climbing the hill on this round planet, getting dizzy on this spinning planet or have wind in our faces on this flying planet?" I put on my best dumbfounded, shocked, stunned look. Or maybe put on my Three Stooges look, since some people have told me that I looked like Larry. I got a consensus from the children that we were all comfortable being duped by our natural home and our natural mother, Mother Earth. Mother Earth wasn't at all like she appeared to be. Nothing is really the way that our senses tell us it ought to be.

"Does anybody know what we call a vision that we see that isn't really there?" I asked getting back into the dialogue. No one knew that answer that I was looking for so I continued. "I'm going to teach you a new word today. The word is mirage. Can we all say, mirage?" I shouted the word. "Now let's say it together. MIRAGE!" I shouted it even louder.

They repeated with more enthusiasm than I expected, "MIRAGE!"

"A mirage is something that we think we see, but it isn't really there. So the flat earth is a mirage and a still earth is a mirage. And now children, let me tell you something else that is a mirage. Death is a mirage. Justin's body died and that is why we are here today and that casket with Justin's body is in the center aisle. But Justin is much more than his body. Justin's spirit and soul and energy of love are alive and will live forever."

"You've all been so good that I want to tell you a story about Justin that you probably don't know. One day Justin had a conversation with his favorite person from the movie, *Toy Story 2*. Do you know who that might be?"

One child blurted out questioningly, "Buzz Lightyear?" I could see the looks of disbelief and even see some eyes roll at the stupidity of the child who had called out.

Now I looked across the aisle where the family was sitting to find Justin's mother, Karen, in the first pew. "Karen, I see some question marks on the faces of Justin's class here. Could you tell me whether Justin ever got to talk to Buzz Lightyear?"

With perky, put-on confidence this crushed mother said, "Oh yes, Justin talked to Buzz."

Now I had the drop jawed, wide-eyed children back in the palm of my hand, where I wanted them. It was time for another question. "Can all of you class tell me together what is the famous line Buzz uses in the movie?"

I hardly had the words out of my mouth and the answer came back, "To infinity and beyond."

"Let's have all the adults join us and say it once more, everyone together," and I led them and directed them in with my right hand. Together we shouted, "To infinity and beyond!"

I continued. "Infinity is never ending and beyond is longer than never ending. Infinity is like the life of Justin's soul, spirit and love life, never ending and more. The reason we know that Justin's life is that long and without end is that Justin was born into the Jesus life in baptism. And so Justin and his parents and family believe that Justin lives to infinity and beyond with Jesus. I invite you all to say that with me once more." I coached them and directed them in for the chorus, "To infinity and beyond with Jesus!"

I was about to conclude, but I wanted to make sure this insight lasted through the worship. "Boys and girls, Justin's family and friends, Immaculate Conception Church family, today we will do something special at the liturgy. At all the times when we usually say AMEN, today we will say, AMEN, TO INFINITY AND BEYOND WITH JESUS." And we said that all one more time. I was excited and practically exhausted. I was energized and overwhelmed by the success of the talk and the insights that I don't think I understood even at the beginning of the preaching. God had worked overtime, but there was still more to do. However, I knew that Justin's tough and tender spirit would guide us as we continued in prayer.

The funeral Mass ended and the crowd filed out of church for an even more difficult task. The music, the words, the close warmth of the community and the soft stained glass ambiance all made the sacramental celebration bearable and even consoling. But to exit into the cold dampness, mud and puddles and the burial itself would present spinal chills anew. The firemen mounted the back of the truck for the second and final Make a Wish ride to the cemetery. I had never been in a funeral procession that was led by a fire truck, and it made the other drivers much more courteous and less challenging than they are at the less unique funerals. While we were at church, the black clouds lightened up and, as we drove to the cemetery, there were a few breaks and bits of blue sky snuck out in streaks. By the time we arrived at the cemetery, the sun was showing through in spots. Where it hit the pedals and the leaves of the gold, purple and yellow hardy mums, there was a show of sparkling crystals in the dangling rain drops. The sun became bolder in its appearance, and the multi-faceted jewels of water dazzled on the grass, shrubs and flowers.

The walk to the grave site was squishy and treacherous but without incident. Pigs would have felt at home, but everyone managed. Blue and white balloons were released to float into the air representing a strong spirit set free. Slowly folks inched away from the burial to regroup once more at an aunt's house for a luncheon. It was lavish and abundant having been prepared by Kevin's catering company that had supported him so graciously throughout the agony of Justin's illness.

I prepared my plate and sat down at the table next to Kevin. As I put the lettuce and pickles on my sandwich, I began the conversation on a high. "Did you notice the streak of sun that appeared as we came into the cemetery and the jeweled rain droplets dangling from the gorgeous hardy mums?"

Much to my surprise, almost shock, Kevin said, "I won't be happy about today until we have a double rainbow like we saw at Uncle Carl's funeral." Uncle Carl had been Justin's favorite uncle and babysitter who had died a shocking death. The double rainbow had made this family tragedy a tad more palatable even though it was almost total devastation for the family. By this time, I knew that I was out of gas and also out of words of inspiration. So I did the only thing that I could do.

I said, "Oh, I think I forgot to get mustard for my sandwich," and I got up and returned to the buffet table and then went to sit someplace less challenging.

The crowd was so huge that many people sat at tables in the garage. As the meal progressed, the ominous clouds that had darkened the morning reappeared. Only this time, they were even blacker and rolled in with tornado speed and blustery winds. Rain pelted down. Drops as big as silver dollars splattered and bounced off the cars parked in the driveway. The garage door was pulled down to half mast to keep people from eating soaked sandwiches. The thunder rolled through like the kids' tale of the angels bowling in heaven.

Suddenly, the rain subsided to a slow drizzle and the clouds cleared revealing some patches of blue. The garage door was raised to witness the weather phenomenon of blue, clear, fall crispness and behold a double rainbow. From the hilltop setting it seemed to go "from infinity to beyond." I rushed out to my car knowing that my camera was under the front seat and positioned myself perfectly to take in the enormity of the display. I didn't have time to make sure that Kevin knew that there was a double rainbow. I had to take advantage of this Kodak moment. Before mustard, he had sounded pretty demanding and specific, but I felt sure that he would be happy. Indeed it was twice as good a display as Noah got at the end of the forty-day flooding. As luck would have it, there was no film in my camera, but the bulk of the mourners had now turned out to be dancers in the street. Uncle Carl's funeral was not going to outdo nephew Justin's. The family that lived in Canvas Cove was witnessing a work of art of supreme scope and magnificence.

I was haunted by the fact that my camera captured no Kodak moment, but delighted that the crowd had celebrated the extravaganza. As I unwound later that evening, Cindy Presler, the Channel 5, NBC meteorologist began her five-minute weather presentation. "Let's begin with some footage caught by our camera man this afternoon in St. Charles. There was this great double rainbow." For a few seconds the screen was full of the scene that I could never have matched with my 35mm camera.

When the news ended at 10:30 p.m. I called Channel 5 and talked to Cindy. I asked if I could have a copy of that footage with a date and a peacock logo on it so that there would never be a doubt in the family that there was a double rainbow on the day of Justin's funeral.

She said, "I will be happy to help you out. It is good that you called immediately at the conclusion of the news cast, because there is hardly anything at a TV station that has a shorter shelf life than yesterday's weather forecast. Who knows what might have happened to this report by tomorrow?"

I guess she was just being honest, but it was quite humble on her part to question the earth-shaking importance of her job. A few days later, the package arrived with a video of the double rainbow with the date and NBC peacock just as I had hoped. I took it to Justin's home on the evening of his birthday in the middle of November. We sang Happy Birthday. I got a present in return that night. For a second time, I was remembered in a youngster's will. I got a DVD of *Toy Story 2*.

KEVIN'S VIEW OF FATHER KLEBA'S IMPACT WITH MY SON.

Just a note about Father Kleba in the eyes of Justin's father. As we know, Father is a very tall man and is the biggest teddy bear you could encounter. This man was kind, understanding, quiet, loving, sharing and many more things. As time went on, Justin and Father became close friends and understood each other's passion. Justin always enjoyed seeing Father come to the house as he knew that he was bring mail for him. I can remember one time Father had stopped in to see my wife and I briefly and Justin was once again stern with Father about his mail. Father had told Justin, "Don't worry; I will get on this right away." Father had five o'clock mass that evening and told the story of what had happened at our home and that he needed some help. Once again, ICD came through and had made some cards and left them on his door step.

Father came by Sunday evening to share his story and share the cards that had been dropped off. I had received messages from parishioners who had attended the five o'clock mass and were overwhelmed by his story and had lent a hand. John, my neighbor, heard about the plea from Father at the five o'clock mass from others and told me how fortunate we were that such a caring man shared his experience with others. I will always be grateful to God for putting Father Kleba in our lives. Even though Justin has gone to be with Jesus, our relationship with Father has continued through the years. Even though he moved from ICD, he still keeps in touch with me. Father Kleba has continued to make an impact on my life.

CHRISTOPHER PAGE

"Coincidence is God's way of remaining anonymous."
Alcoholics Anonymous

WHILE SOME OF MY FONDNESS FOR YOUNGSTERS is as ordinary as holding hands with Clair, I have another young friend whose name begins with "C" whose life depended on an internationally famous physician. All five-year-olds take their tumbles and have a lot to learn about balance and dexterity, especially in sports. But some are prodigies in sports the way Mozart was in music. Christopher was a boy who fell into that category. Consequently, when he began to tumble down the steps and trip himself while running after a ball in the yard, it was noticeable to his family. As a matter of fact, his dad, had a lot of time on his hands and noticed more about his son at this particular age than he really would have liked. Bob Page, Chris' dad, had recently lost his job and was spending a lot of time at home with his family that included his wife Sandy, and Chris' older brother, Michael. Bob's unemployment tripped him up as a father, husband and provider just as Chris' clumsiness tripped him up.

Sometimes kids like to fall and roll around on the grass, but Christopher was suddenly losing his balance and getting angry at himself because he could not walk smoothly and run with agility. Physical frustration was not typical for this energetic boy with an athletic stature. When a visit to the family doctor uncovered nothing regarding his problem, Bob took him to St. Louis Children's Hospital for a more thorough examination. A brain scan there revealed a sizable tumor on Chris's brain. Further testing and consultation led to the conclusion that Chris needed to have brain surgery. This first tragedy was followed by another horrible setback. Since Children's Hospital did not take the limited insurance that Bob had in his unemployed state, he was told to take his son to Cardinal Glennon Hospital for Children.

It was at this time that I was invited into the Page family home. The Pages were just one of many new families in this sprawling subdivision area served by Immaculate Conception Parish in Dardenne Prairie, MO. I drove to a subdivision that was so new I had never noticed it before.

When I arrived, I met a vibrant couple who were still reeling from their son, Christopher's recent terrible medical diagnosis. Both Christopher and Michael were outside playing. Bob and Sandy had sent them outside so we could talk privately.

After the usual introductions, they apologized for not introducing themselves to me in church. I told them that with thirteen Masses on the weekend, three worship sites and 3,200 families, I was still getting to know people. I understood the snarled parking lot was an encouragement for people to leave quickly and make room for those attending the next Mass. It would take me some time to get to know everyone so it was good to have this opportunity today. That was small talk, pleasantries to break the ice. Now we knew we had to get to the heart of the matter, the "c" words: Chris' cancer.

"Father, we're new here. We barely got settled, and now Bob has lost the job that brought us to St. Louis. We're really in a bind. Christopher is our youngest son and is only five years old. He just started to act clumsy, and it took us awhile to decide that he wasn't merely putting on an act like an apprentice circus clown. So, to just cut to the chase, we went to St. Louis Children's Hospital and were told that Chris needs brain surgery on a sizable tumor. We were told that our medical insurance wouldn't be accepted by that hospital. They said we would have to go somewhere else. So we want to know if you know anyone at the Catholic children's hospital called Cardinal Glennon because we don't want to go there and get the same bad news twice."

Bob chimed in, "I feel like such a failure without a job and adequate health insurance at the very time that my family needs me the most." His anguish verged on tears. The move to St. Louis wasn't supposed to be the beginning of a life of trauma.

Wow, that was a mouthful of hard stuff that would devastate the strongest parents. "Before I answer your question, I have to tell you how sorry I am about your little boy and about your bad fortune in losing a job that just brought you to our city. I sure hope that you have some success in your job hunt. But I know you want some information about Cardinal Glennon Children's Hospital. I think I can put some of your worries to rest. I have been a priest in St. Louis for over thirty years, and during that time, I have spent most of my years serving in poor parishes in the heart of the city. On several occasions, I have been approached by people who had accumulated huge bills at Cardinal Glennon Hospital. These people were extremely poor. They were petrified to think that the bill collector was going to be at their door forcing them to declare bankruptcy or that they would be evicted for non-payment of rent. There was also the fear that they would have their modest paycheck garnished for non-payment of debts. In all of these cases, I called the hospital and explained the situation and in every instance I was told to have the people come to the billing office to work out some kind of payment plan. I have never heard of these people being mistreated or dunned by a bill collector, but rather I have seen everyone treated with respect and understanding. The comment the billing office always makes is, 'We certainly hope that this family thinks that our service to their child was worth something and that they are willing to make some sacrifice. In that case, we are more than happy to work with them.' So having said all that, I want to encourage you to take Chris to Cardinal Glennon Hospital with confidence; get their medical diagnosis and then see how they can help. I'm sure money and insurance will not be an issue."

I drew a breath at the end of my long narrative, but I could also see them exhale with some amount of relief although they were still in emotional knots over the gravity of Chris' problem. "Now get Chris a referral to Cardinal Glennon and get the ball rolling without delay."

Due to the severity of his situation, Chris was able to be seen in two days and got a complete evaluation. The briefest explanation confirmed that Chris had a tumor just as they had already been told. However, the treatment schedule laid out by Cardinal Glennon called for no surgery, but rather for an intensive radiation schedule. Yes, Cardinal Glennon would take Bob's health insurance. That was good news, but certainly ambiguous to say the least. It was wonderful to know that Chris' situation would not put them out on the street when the bills came. That was true if they chose Cardinal Glennon and believed their treatment plan to be best. However, it was unclear which hospital and treatment was better. His parents were left wondering how to decide.

If one studies the AMA listings of fine hospitals, it is likely that St. Louis Children's Hospital will show up on the top rankings more frequently than Cardinal Glennon Hospital will. If you look at the medical schools to which each is attached, Washington University for Children's will be ranked higher than St. Louis University's Medical School, which serves Cardinal Glennon. So on both of those counts, the better choice is the hospital that doesn't take Bob's insurance. This was a dilemma that no one wanted to face. No parent wants to make a life and death decision regarding his or her child on a flip of a coin. So where does that leave a family in distress?

It was time to have a powwow of the entire clan. The Page family was from the Pittsburgh area and had parents and other relatives there. Chris' wrenching health news and the shock of Bob's job loss brought family members to the Midwest to lend their support and shared wisdom. On the following Sunday afternoon, one of the uncles got off the plane and had the solution to the problem in the palm of his hand. He was carrying a copy of *Think Big* by Dr. Ben Carson.

Uncle Al kept the book hidden until he was in the family living room. Then he cleared his throat and got the attention of the family. "God brought me an answer to our prayers today and I can't wait to tell you all about it. Let me show you this book that I read on the plane during my trip here from Pittsburgh. I picked up this book at the airport. It's written by a doctor named Ben Carson. It practically jumped off the rack into my hand when I was actually looking for a candy bar. Anyway, he is the head of pediatric neurosurgery at Johns Hopkins University Hospital in Baltimore. He was the doctor in charge of overseeing the successful separation of two Siamese twins who were joined at the brain. He had seventy doctors working under him during that surgery. In the book he tells the story of a boy named 'Christopher' who was in our Chris' situation. He saved that Christopher's life.

He's the best in the world. We have to get Chris to Baltimore so that Dr. Carson can look at him and tell us what to do. I say we just get Chris into the hands of the best doctor and let him do the surgery that St. Louis Children's Hospital recommends."

Then it was rebuttal time. "That might be a good idea, but how do we know that he will take him as a patient, and how much will that cost us?"

That was an important consideration, but there was a prevailing notion that Uncle Al was on to something and that it was divine providence that he found Dr. Carson's book at the airport. Everyone agreed that the family was in dire need of a sign from God. *Think Big* was quite an extraordinary possibility. When the situation is impossible it is important to look at every possibility and not discount any option. It was important to "think big."

Bob invited me to the house to meet the family. He felt I was now a part of the family. He couldn't wait for my arrival to tell me the breakthrough thinking that had transpired over the last hour with Uncle Al introducing Ben Carson into the mix. So he mentioned Dr. Carson's book while we talked on the phone. If it was confusing with just the two St. Louis hospital choices, then why not add to it by throwing Baltimore's best doctor and most likely the world's best pediatric neurosurgeon into the equation?

When he paused for a moment, I told him I was eager to come and I would be right over. And then I added, "Believe me, when I arrive, I'll bring more to the table than just a good appetite. I might bring a miracle."

I couldn't wait to get to the house. When I arrived, I shook hands all around and got to work with my chapter of the unfolding saga.

"I have to tell you all that I think Dr. Ben Carson's involvement is a great idea and might be easier than you could ever imagine. I invited Ben Carson to St. Louis this week and will be having dinner with him on Friday evening." I could sense the wide-eyed disbelief and heard an audible gasp.

"You what? Where is the Friday night dinner? I'll be there!" Sandy blurted this out with a hopeful light in her eyes and a fist pump to highlight it.

"Yes," I started over again now with more specificity. "I am part of a group that invited Dr. Carson to come to St. Louis to make a presentation about the Dr. Ben Carson Scholarship Fund. We are going to start a chapter here in St. Louis to match the ones already operating in Baltimore, Detroit, and Philadelphia. We have invited some people together for an evening presentation to kick things off. We will have the gathering at a downtown bank's executive dining room. Now even in the few moments that I have had to think since I got your phone call, I have to say that it's not clear to me how scholarship fund presentations and brain scans come together. So let's think about it and talk some more this evening. Then I will call some of the others on the committee to see how they think we might proceed. They will certainly understand the gravity of the situation, but we also have to know that Dr. Carson is coming to St. Louis to talk scholarships and not brain surgery."

A few phone calls the next day had the ball rolling and gave me some direction on behalf of the Page Family. The Pages were assured by Cardinal Glennon Hospital that Dr. Carson would be welcome to use all of their facilities to study the image of Chris' brain and collaborate with the doctors on staff there about the radiation treatments they recommended.

My conversation with the Scholarship Foundation in Baltimore was clear, but not immediately hopeful. They said, "When Dr. Carson comes to a city to talk about scholarships, he doesn't come to talk about sick children and brain surgery. Every time Dr. Carson turns around, there are people who have some medical issue to talk about. It doesn't even have to be about children or neurology; they just want to talk over some personal health concern with a world-renowned physician. So when he comes to St. Louis, he is not coming to talk about Christopher Page. We would appreciate it if you would not pester him about that matter, urgent as it is. We will speak to him, and if he wants to involve himself in this child's problem, he won't go to Cardinal Glennon anyway. Whenever he goes to another hospital he knows that he is treated like a celebrity. That treatment makes him uncomfortable. Besides, he really does trust and respect the folks on his team at Johns Hopkins. So at best he might agree to have the family send all of Christopher's scans to him in Baltimore. He will then study them with his team and give his opinion in his own surroundings."

It wasn't all that I wanted to hear, but it was quite encouraging and certainly didn't slam the door in Chris' face.

Friday night arrived; it was time for the Carson Scholarship Fund Dinner. Bob accompanied me to the reception before dinner. I introduced Bob as a friend who was interested in hearing more about the program. Dr. Carson barely heard his name and said, "Oh, you're the man whose son has the brain tumor. I'm happy to meet you. I am sad about your son."

We were both shocked and wondered whether this great doctor was able to read concern by looking at the worry lines on Bob's face. We assumed that his staff had warned him in advance about the great concern of a St. Louis parent, and so he remembered the name. We reassured ourselves that we had kept our word about not bringing up any medical matter. We hadn't; Dr. Carson had.

Dr. Carson continued, "Send me all the scans. When I get back to the hospital, I will visit with my staff and give you our best evaluation of the problem and the way that you might proceed with your son." He continued somewhat apologetically, "You have to understand that there are always people who want to talk to me about matters even if they are not in my area of expertise. Once I had a man come to me who was an Arab oil sheik. He told me that if I would operate on his wife's brain tumor, he would give me one billion dollars to build a new hospital. I told him that I was an expert in pediatric surgery, that I never operated on adults, and that I am sure that he could find someone competent in that field who would be happy to have his generous support. When people are ill, they would give all of their money to get better. Good health is worth everything."

Bob didn't have any money, but I knew that he was in total agreement. I'm not sure how much he heard about the workings of the scholarship program as it was explained that evening. I do know that he heard the sentence about sending Chris' scans to Johns-Hopkins. As we walked to our car, Bob recalled Dr. Carson' story about turning down an offer to operate for one billion dollars. "Who ever heard anything like that? No one could ever call him greedy."

By the end of the next week, Ben Carson had studied the scans and was back in touch with the Pages. His opinion was that he would never do surgery and agreed totally with the Cardinal Glennon evaluation and treatment plan. "Don't come to Baltimore, because I would never operate on your son. Go to Cardinal Glennon and take the radiation therapy that they prescribe. That is exactly the right thing to do, and they are very capable of doing it. We would not serve you any better at Johns-Hopkins." What a relief. All of their skepticism was now relieved, replaced with real hope. They had to replace the terror in their lives with hope and peaceful confidence that they were doing the best thing and going to the best hospital.

The preliminary task before beginning the actual radiation treatment was to make a custom fitted helmet for Chris that would assure the radiation laser struck the tumor perfectly. I never saw it, but I had to surmise that it looked something like a modern version of the medieval helmet worn by the Knights of the Round Table. It had a pin hole in exactly the place where the x-rays would penetrate the tumor with microscopic precision. Once this was fabricated, Chris had to go to the hospital twice a week for radiation. It required him to put on this helmet, get his head bolted securely to a steel table in the radiation center, and then have the x-rays directed into the pin hole at the precise angle to kill the cancer. The preparation with the fitting of the helmet and the bolting to the table took longer than the actual treatment. Every visit to the hospital was a day to miss school; Chris was always ready for that. After a while he become so fond of the nurses, the family stopped at Krispy Kreme for donuts to take to the hospital for the staff. Chris got to eat one along the way.

I stayed in touch with the family by phone regularly, and I went out to the house many evenings to see Chris and pray with the family. Chris' grandmother stayed during those months, and we became friends. Sometimes when I was ready to go home, Chris would come and give me a hug. More than once Sandy said in exasperated frustration, "Chris, I don't get it. You give him a hug and you never give your mother a hug." We laughed and Chris gave a coy grin as he ran up to bed. He was quick, but his balance was uncertain.

I doubt whether that was the whole truth, but if it was I'm sure that Sandy imparted a few hugs and kisses when she went up to check on Chris in the middle of the night. After some months, Chris got stronger and Cardinal Glennon pronounced him healed. This was at about the same time that Bob, got a new job at the renowned Carnegie Hotel, an historic treasure in Pittsburgh. So there was joy and incomprehensible riches before all the money ran out. We had a celebration for both the job and the healing, but I'm sure that everyone viewed Chris' new life as the bigger miracle.

Once more, parting was sad, but at least it was not a parting from life in this world. The path from tragedy to redemption from death to life will seldom be celebrated with greater joy even in church on Easter Sunday morning. Over the years, I received Christmas card photos featuring a smiling, handsome Chris. These photos and occasional phone calls assured me of the family's gratitude as well as Chris's growth and good health.

In 2011, ten years later, Ben Carson was coming to St. Louis to be part of the annual St. Louis Speaker Series. During those intervening years, there had still not been a successful effort on behalf of the

Ben Carson Scholarship Fund. I called the Pages on the day of his talk to tell Sandy that I needed an update on Chris' health in case I could get backstage to talk with Dr. Carson. When his presentation was over, I wandered backstage at Powell Symphony Hall and found the door ajar. I mentioned to the security guard that I was an old acquaintance of Dr. Carson, and he directed me to his dressing room. Dr. Carson is small in stature for such a big man. He brimmed with warmth and charm. He was eager to hear of Chris' excellent health, soccer prowess, and good grades, the kind of achievements that might qualify a boy for a Ben Carson Scholarship. He said, "Tell the family that I am happy to hear the news and that I wish them a Merry Christmas."

I concluded that destiny didn't bring Dr. Carson to St. Louis in 2002 to usher in a scholarship program, because that didn't happen. The dinner meeting and talk that night in 2002 didn't stir up the support I had hoped for. I couldn't even get the Catholic educators I invited to attend. In looking back, I don't think that was the focal point of the evening. Ben Carson was to come and be the brilliant diagnostician for a stumbling little boy and his heartsick parents. He was to be the unseen hand that pulled together the threads of information to make a beautiful tapestry of healthy energy. He was to balance out the ragged tatters of contradiction and broken heartedness in the Page family.

Lord Acton said, "There is no greater power than the power of an idea whose time has come." Ten years later, the time for the Ben Carson Scholarship Foundation idea has not yet arrived for St. Louis. However, ten years prior, the idea of Dr. Ben Carson's healing insight was right on time for Christopher Page.

BOB AND SANDY PAGE, CHRIS'S PARENTS, SAY

During a time that was very difficult for our family, Fr. Kleba came into our lives and helped open our eyes to a deeper faith. There were so many things that happened during the time of our son's illness that could not really be explained, that we were very certain that God was truly present in our lives, in a much more affirmative way than we had ever felt previously. We felt that God truly sent Fr. Kleba to us to help us to deal with the tragic news that we had been given regarding our son. We invited him into our home, and prayed with him each time he came, and this always made us feel stronger, to deal with the challenging diagnosis with which we had been presented. Our son Christopher was a very shy child, but ironically, not with Fr. Kleba. We could not figure it out, as he would give Fr. Kleba hugs, when he was not always so quick to offer them to us, his parents. He always got a smile on his face when he knew that Fr. Kleba was coming to the house to see him. Through all of the events throughout our ordeal, we look back on what transpired, and I tell the story to many people, how I now feel that there is certainly a great presence from God, and I utilize this whenever I can to inspire others to have faith and to realize that there is always hope. We will be forever grateful to Fr. Gerry Kleba for the friendship, and spiritual guidance that he provided to us in this time of need.

Saint Cronan Community

AT ST. CRONAN'S MY FEAR was of people angry with the institutional church who were outspoken in their intelligent critique of the abuse situation. My predecessor was an abusive priest and the church had paid off his accusers and covered up for him prior to his arrival at St. Cronan's. I entered a volatile hornets' nest. My additional fear was that I had to walk a tightrope, sometimes even a jumping rope, with one foot in the hierarchical, institutional church and the other foot in the People of God Church called the St. Cronan Community. The parish had been officially designated the "personal parish for people dedicated to the social justice of the gospel" by Archbishop Raymond Burke. This title appeared to be a miracle programmed by the Holy Spirit Herself, because Burke was on the far right and St. Cronan's outside the lines on the far left.

Members of the St. Cronan Community called Cronanites were committed to all of the social issues and 'isms' that plague our world. They felt as motivated to protest injustice within the church as they were to go to the streets protesting war. As a member of the clergy and the pastor of this social justice parish, I was torn. One birthday, I received the gift of a baseball hat with two bills, one going out to the right and the other to the left; in the center it read, "I am their leader, which way did they go?" I continued to hope, praying as my spiritual director had advised me: "God, give Raymond all he needs." This former Benedictine Abbot said, "We all know that Raymond Burke is a very needy person, but we should best leave it to God to know exactly what he needs." I prayed those seven syllables hundreds of times a day and invited anyone who cared to join me in the petition.

When the stress was almost unbearable, my life was further complicated. I was diagnosed with fourth stage lung cancer, told that it was fast spreading, and that it was incurable. When it seemed that I was languishing, hanging on by a frayed thread, two more miracles transformed my life. A second opinion from Memorial Sloan-Kettering Cancer Center in New York proved that I had been misdiagnosed. I thanked God and used my lungs battered by a year of chemotherapy to breathe a sigh of relief. Secondly, Archbishop Burke was promoted to a higher office in the Vatican, which was what both God and Burke knew he needed. This time, I used my lungs to sing the Alleluia Chorus, sotto voce, of course. With Burke leaving, his threat of suspension was removed. I dismissed the canon lawyer who was defending me.

Saint Louis was blessed with the appointment of a new archbishop, a servant leader named Bob Carlson. This appointment allowed me to breathe more easily as I had frequently found myself under scrutiny and judgment from the far right. Carlson and I have prayed together personally and he has even knelt at my feet and asked for my blessing.

"BE SHEPHERDS LIVING WITH THE SMELL OF THE SHEEP"

Pope Francis said, "May we never remain on the sidelines of this march of living hope! Because we do not always see these seeds growing, we need an interior certainty, a conviction that God is able to act in every situation, even amid apparent setbacks: "we have this treasure in earthen vessels" (2 Cor 4:7). This certainty is often called "a sense of mystery." It involves knowing with certitude that all those who entrust themselves to God in love will bear good fruit (cf. JN 15:5). This fruitfulness is often invisible, elusive and unquantifiable." Ibid. *Evangelii Guadium.* p. 192.

In the *National Catholic Reporter*, Joan Barthel wrote:
"ST. LOUIS — When Fr. Gerald Kleba volunteered to take over as pastor of St. Cronan Parish 10 years ago, he walked into a devastated parish. Its former pastor, Joe Ross, was a pedophile. Even though he had pleaded guilty to kissing a boy in confession, and had been arrested twice on other charges of sexual misconduct, the St. Louis archdiocese had shuffled him from parish to parish until he was sent to St. Cronan, where he was pastor for 11 years.

"Oh God, the anger of the people here!" Kleba recalled. "I never knew what a hornet's nest I was getting into. People were angry at Joe Ross, angry at the archbishop for sending him here, angry at me because they couldn't trust that the archdiocese wasn't screwing them again."

The people were not only angry, but resentful. They had wanted to hire a rota of priests for one year, while they collectively considered the next step.

"Coming here was the greatest humbling experience of my life," Kleba said. "The first week, I was told to just sit in a pew in the middle of the church until the people could do a blessing over me and welcome me into being their pastor. I felt very second-rate."

A devastated parish will either drift into irrelevance, or it will pick up the pieces and try to put itself back together. St. Cronan shows how a parish with a determined pastor and an involved laity can not only survive a pedophile priest, but can rebuild itself into what the pastor calls "the church of the future."

It begins with the brochure at the church's front door: "All are welcome: young, old; gay, straight; rich, poor; Catholic or not." At Sunday Mass, a lesbian couple and their children walk up the aisle and offer the gifts. At the Eucharist, people surround the altar. They do not simply say amen; in a climate invigorated with the adrenaline of the Second Vatican Council, the pastor opens his arms: *Let the church say amen.*

Kleba, who prefers to be called Gerry — "I'm not much into clericalism" — stresses lay leadership. "There's a high level of shared responsibility and equality here, and since I encourage it, people give more of themselves. For several years I didn't even write a reflection in the bulletin, because I didn't want people to feel that this is the pastor's thing."

He lives in a pleasant, old-fashioned house next to the small church, a modest red-brick building that has no funds for air-conditioning in the city's scalding summers. "Raising money takes a major effort," Gerry said. "Many people here don't believe in the diocesan church. They don't want to contribute to a seminary that doesn't take women."

It's a mostly white parish in a district that's mostly black, and it has a high percentage of professionals: teachers and social workers, some doctors and lawyers, a circuit court judge. "It's a very complex group of people," longtime parishioner Tom Mullen said. "They're thinkers, which always gets you in trouble."

At 70, Gerry's had both a knee and a hip replacement, but he rides his bike and swims at the Y. He takes piano lessons, paints landscapes, and has written three books: *The People Parish: A Model of Church Where People Flourish, Joseph Remembered: The Father of Jesus* and *Why Go to Mass?* He's donated 225 pints of blood and has pestered other people into doing the same. "Other priests ask for money," a parishioner said. "Gerry asks for blood."

He always wanted to be a priest. In eighth grade, he had to write an essay on "Why a Religious Vocation Appeals to Me." That was in 1955, when the Catholic church and its schoolteachers described the priesthood in uncomplicated, sentimental terms. "I believe it is the simplest, surest and shortest way to heaven," he wrote. He won third prize.

Beginning with the seminary, he knew it would not be simple. "It was boot camp -- belittling, dictatorial and non-intellectual, but it was the only way to get to the priesthood." He was ordained in 1967, setting out on a priestly path that has taken him from a country parish to the University of Notre Dame to the suburbs to the inner city, where he confronted racism, including his own. "I had known only a few black people in my life, and I was scared. I was afraid of people standing on street corners, afraid to knock on neighbors' doors." He was yelled at: "Get your white ass out of this neighborhood!" A black parishioner told him how her son, walking in a white section of the city, had stopped at a church to go to confession. "For your penance," the priest told him, "never set foot in this church again."

By 2004, two years into his pastorate at St. Cronan, the pastoral team consisted of Gerry, a gay man and a nun. "A woman and a gay man as copastors bring authenticity to who they are," he said. "They are people baptized in the priesthood of Christ Jesus. The Catholic church can violate people's rights as much as, say, the Chinese Communist Party."

But Archbishop Raymond Burke had come to town in 2003. He made national headlines by declaring that he would deny Communion to any pro-choice Catholic politician, and that any Catholic who voted for such a candidate would be guilty of serious sin. And he set about cracking down on St. Cronan, with special focus on the nun, Charity Sr. Louise Lears.

Known as a compassionate, faith-filled woman, Lears taught a college class in the spirituality of nonviolence and helped set up the Center for Victims of Torture and War Trauma. In November 2007, she attended the ordination of two women in the Roman Catholic Women-priests movement at a synagogue that had always had good relations with St. Cronan. Other Catholics had attended the ordination, but a videotape singled Lears out. In December, she received from Burke, by messenger, a canonical admonition, informing her that she was suspected of having committed a grave violation of church teachings and law.

Soon afterward, Gerry was summoned to the archbishop's house. Burke pointed out the priest's shortcomings, but basically his message boiled down to: Fire Lears.

"Archbishop," Gerry said, "I urge you to call Sister Louise and invite her to come here and speak with you personally, rather than have couriers and canon lawyers and juridical hearings. In terms of the Gospel, if your sister or brother has anything against you, leave your gift at the altar and go to that person and be reconciled, then take your gift to the altar."

"Well, if she is willing to come and be reconciled, of course," Burke said.

"Archbishop," Gerry said, "listen again. The Gospel says you go and be reconciled — it doesn't say anything about the other person. I'm not telling you how things will proceed with Sister—I'm only saying that if you talk, something wonderful might happen."

They did not talk. On June 26, 2008, Burke signed an interdict against the nun, accusing her of publicly inciting "animosity or hatred" toward him and the pope. He banished her from ministry in St. Louis and barred her from receiving the sacraments.

On Aug. 10, 2008, St. Cronan held a farewell Mass for her. She packed up her books and her calico cat and moved to Baltimore.

A week later, Burke celebrated his farewell Mass at the cathedral. He moved to Rome, where he became a cardinal and the head of the Vatican's Supreme Court — the very office that would hear any appeal from Lears and her canon lawyers.

That December, Gerry was told he had nonsmoker's lung cancer, stage four, incurable. While he remained St. Cronan's pastor, he moved back to his boyhood home to stay with his sister.

People worried that St. Cronan might be closed. Most Sundays, the little church was only half-filled. Many people had left because of Ross, many more because of the treatment of Lears. Now, in Gerry's absence — nearly a year — a group of parishioners met to figure out: What do we do now? An obvious need was for priests to say Mass, so the parish secretary, a Jesuit who sings in the choir, and other volunteers set out to enlist men who would approve of progressive liturgy and inclusive language. Most Sundays, a priest was available, but once, when the visiting priest could be there for only one of the two Masses, a laywoman led a Communion service. The liturgy committee talked: Should there be only one Mass on Sundays, not two?

People tried to keep things humming, but by the spring of 2009, the parish council had to hire a pastoral associate to pick up the slack. Her job ranged from the simple to the special: seeing to the bread, wine and linens for the liturgies; pre-baptismal conferences with new parents; and, in general, keeping communication open among all the volunteers. To maintain neighborhood outreach, the social justice committee organized a Community Building Day: Men and women hit the streets to paint, repair fences and broken steps, and do simple carpentry work. Another team planned a major auction, to be held in the large auditorium of a nearby church; that event netted $31,000, a financial godsend.

Gerry had 12 months of chemotherapy and the tumors didn't go away, but he wasn't dead either. He got a second opinion and learned the diagnosis was a mistake: He never had lung cancer, but a white blood cell disorder. Even without treatment, he could live with it for 20 or 30 years.

Buoyed by this news, he invited the new archbishop, Robert Carlson, to come to St. Cronan. Not all parishioners were happy with the invitation. Although Carlson had not been in St. Louis at the time of Ross, he represented the hierarchical church that had sent a known pedophile to them. Before the archbishop came to celebrate Eucharist, they wanted to clear the air.

On May 1, 2010, Gerry and a dozen parishioners met with the archbishop at his house. A member of the parish council described the experiences people had had with the temperamental Ross. "We saw his anger and his lack of cooperation, but that did not indicate to us that there was a deeper problem."

"He would ask kids to the rectory, then up to his room to have a beer," another woman said. One girl later told her mother that when she went into the private reconciliation room, he had her sit on his lap. "Children relate to the image of the Good Shepherd," the woman continued. "The Good Shepherd protects. Now the sacraments are destroyed for our children. My son said to me, 'Being a priest is worse than being a garbage collector.'" She began to cry.

"It goes beyond Joe Ross," a man said. "It's systemic." He said that a priest had abused him, and the check that the St. Louis archdiocese sent to reimburse him for therapy was drawn on a bank in Iowa. "That's a form of secrecy," he said, looking intently at the archbishop. "I pray you can be a cure for this disease."

"We've just scratched the surface," Carlson said. "We've begun a journey. What's the next step? I don't know. When I was ordained 40 years ago, I had all the answers."

"He was put in our parish without our full knowledge," a woman said, "and he was removed without explanation. That encouraged a feeling of mistrust."

"The archdiocese did not handle this well," Carlson said. "On behalf of the church, I apologize."

Six weeks later, when Carlson came to St. Cronan to celebrate Mass, he spoke privately with the family of a girl who said Ross had abused her when she was 10. Some people were unhappy that he had not apologized publicly; other parishioners thought that just having the archbishop come where no archbishop had come for years was in itself an apology.

Gerry had a positive take on the archbishop's visit: "Actions speak louder than words."

At the barbecue after Mass, the archbishop drank beer from a bottle and stood in line at the makeshift buffet table in Gerry's garage to fix his own plate from the array of grilled bratwurst, hamburgers and hot dogs, chocolate cake and cherry pie. No special place had been reserved for him; he found a seat and chatted with people around him. One man offered to join him in the evenings when the archbishop walks his dogs.

Gerry was smiling. "All these years, I kept thinking, I just want some harmony here. Now I think we've turned a vital corner. St. Cronan's is going to flourish. It's a new day. The sun will shine again."

February 17 - March 1, 2012

JEREMIAH TRUETKEN-BUSIEK

"It is the absurdity of family life,
the raggedness of it,
that is at once its redemption and its true nobility."
James McBride, author and musician.

I HAD RECENTLY BEEN ASSIGNED as pastor of St. Cronan Parish when I called the secretary to inform her that I was coming to visit. I had met Delores once before, and I was immediately aware that, given her many years of service, she was competent and confident. She had been at the parish for fifteen years, enduring much through the horrors of the abusive previous pastor. While not physically abusive to her, he had been verbally and emotionally threatening, one minute showing her the door over some trivial item and then begging her to stay. The fact that she tolerated this nonsense marked her as a strong woman able to stand her ground with valor and never be mistaken for a shrinking violet. At the same time Delores Blount, a wife and mother of two daughters, was as sensitive and empathic as a professional counselor. She is exactly the person that any church worthy of the gospel needs at the front desk, answering the door, greeting folks and listening with the third ear of the heart. Hence it is easy to understand why Delores would have given me this directive during my first encounter with her. Fortunately, I was wise enough to listen and give her the first impression that I was docile. It helped to smooth the waves of turbulence left in the wake of the previous pastor's removal.

"Father, it's fine if you want to come here and visit today, but if you want to get your stay at St. Cronan's off to the best possible start, I'll tell you what you should do." There wasn't time for me to assure her that I wanted to get my ministry off to a great start, because she rambled on. "There's a seven-year-old boy named Jeremiah Busiek who has a brain tumor, and he is getting operated on at Cardinal Glennon Hospital as we speak. If you went there to meet his family, and sat with them and prayed, they would be really appreciative."

I thought, "No one can accuse her of being shy, tentative or non-directive." That was all I needed to know, so after she gave me the names and proper spelling of his parents and his only sister, I was off to the hospital. The hospital was only a mile from the parish so it was great pastoral advice and didn't even take me out of the way. Even though I had been a priest for thirty-five years and had performed more than my share of ministry to sick children, the sadness and anxiety that prevail in these situations is never something I can accept. I arrived at Cardinal Glennon Children's Hospital, a landmark for St. Louis Catholics, because it was the first Catholic children's hospital in the U.S. I decided to visit the chapel first before meeting the distressed family. I walked by the huge chrome letters on a long hallway proclaiming "Bob Costas Cancer Center." The St. Louis celebrity and NBC Olympic broadcaster was one of the most visible supporters of the hospital, having raised untold millions in his annual fundraising galas that had been a tradition for over twenty years. As I walked down the corridor, I wondered how close the work they were doing there might come to curing Jeremiah's brain cancer.

I found the chapel, which appeared to be hidden away in a far corner, but then I realized that it was probably more central in the original configuration of the hospital. With the many wings and additions, it was no longer on the beaten path. The visit to the hospital chapel was worth the trip not only for its peace and solitude, but also for the magnificent mural of Jesus with as diverse a group of children and animals as one could find. A painted bubbling river ran through the middle of the mural, symbolizing life and nourishment, enhanced the scene. Kids were playing and dangling their feet in the water as they sat on a rock wall along the bank, watching the fish in the pristine stream.

After catching my breath, I settled in and reflected on my own dread and insecurity about walking in to meet this family in such a fragile situation. I breathed deeply and realized I was carrying more baggage than a barge being pushed by a Mississippi River towboat. I wondered about the welcome I would receive from Jeremiah's family. Would they see me as a Jesus person or a diabolical intruder? I would have traded this moment for my original plans of meeting Delores, checking out my new digs at the rectory, and getting her take on parish life in the wake of the removal of the previous pastor.

I refocused by looking at the mural and Jesus with the excited, playful children. I began to pray for Jeremiah's healing by the touch of the warm, alive Jesus with the joyful giddy kids. I prayed that the family I would meet would be somewhat composed and not too angry and inconsolable. I prayed for the research going on at the Costas Center that they would find an answer to Jeremiah's problem. I prayed for the heartsick parents who were named Mary and Gary. I prayed for grandparents who always question God's math at a time like this as they wonder why they are so healthy and their young grandson so stricken. I prayed for doctors doing the delicate surgery where they may have little likelihood to cure and constantly worry that a tiny miscue could paralyze or even kill. I prayed for myself that I might be a peaceful, hopeful presence in this situation.

Here I was presenting myself out of the blue to these people who knew nothing about me. They knew that their previous pastor had been removed because he was a child abuser. I was an unknown entity walking in at the time of their child's greatest need and vulnerability. I too was anguished not knowing if I would be welcomed and embraced as a healing presence or found questionable, maybe even despicable, because of the stain of abuse and the cloud of questioning about the integrity of any man who wore a black suit and Roman collar. Now that I was here, I questioned the wisdom of Delores in giving me this as my first parish assignment.

The quandary continued. Maybe I should have gone to the church office and looked over the financial report or gone to my bedroom and moved some furniture, but this visiting a sick child might not have been an appropriate opening act for me on the new stage at St. Cronan's. But here I was. I had to pry myself out of the comfortable quiet of the chapel and go to the parents' waiting room. I gathered my courage, took a deep breath, genuflected and went in search of the surgery section. As I walked the brightly decorated halls, I felt like a walking paradox; hoping to promote peace and healing, but possibly to be viewed as a threat and unwelcome intruder. My stomach rumbled and I wanted to stop in the bathroom, but I suspected that was just one psychosomatic delaying tactic and there might be others that would keep me from facing the situation. I followed the signs to the surgical waiting room and went in to introduce myself to strangers. I whispered my name around the room to the gathered families and finally got to those who were Jeremiah's grandparents, parents and some aunts.

While the introductions were subdued as appropriate for the place, it seemed that everyone was delighted to meet me and pleased that Delores had so properly prioritized my life on my first day at St. Cronan's. They felt confident that the doctor had been honest in preparing them for the procedure and hopeful about its likely outcome. We prayed together and sat to visit and idle away the time. We talked about my history of assignments in the priesthood. I learned what parishes and neighborhoods they called home. Mary and Gary told me that they had moved out of the parish area and now lived about twenty miles away at St. Joseph Parish in Imperial, MO. However, they still felt a kinship with St. Cronan's and our ecumenical openness and social justice concerns. Gary worked with the homeless at the Salvation Army. Ecumenism was a daily reality for him. Mary had served at an Indian mission with the Jesuit Volunteers and developed a great sense of the Native American spirituality. She found many like-minded folks at St. Cronan's, where a large percentage of members had done volunteer service in poverty areas.

When I left, I felt so welcomed by the family. I experienced such a sense of prayer and hospitality that I wondered why I had ever been so anxious and painted such a gloomy picture. Someone once said, "Growth is the only evidence of life." I had grown through this situation and had to remind myself once more not to be such a crepe hanger. I walked to the parking garage silently singing Delores' praises and feeling a warm St. Cronan welcome.

Jeremiah got better after this surgery and enjoyed a level of good health in the wilderness that surrounded his family's new home in the country. It was on a steep hill, bounded on one side by the Mastodon State Park, which had a museum and nature center that boasted images of the larger than elephant-sized creatures that roamed the Mississippi Valley thousands of years ago. The mastodons were extinct and the primitive people's thatched-roof huts had disappeared and been replaced with subdivisions. The Busiek family home was unique being alone in the woods where the creeks still ran and the Ozark rock outcroppings scarred the earth. It was closer to the American Indian experience than it was to the red brick tightly squeezed homes and blocks in St. Cronan's neighborhood. Sometimes the family attended Mass at St. Cronan's, but their children went to St. Joseph School. The trip to our church was an hour-long Sunday drive. Everyone was happy to see the family when they came, but Jeremiah's health situation didn't allow them the luxury of the journey to the city very often.

Over the next year Jeremiah's health worsened and he needed to return to the hospital. The room was cramped and often either Mary or Gary stayed overnight. Even though the Ronald McDonald House was only two blocks away, Jeremiah wanted the companionship and both parents felt like the house ought to be reserved for people who traveled greater distances than they did. The reclining chair in the hospital room was not even a reasonable facsimile of the brand name Lazy Boy. It did recline but only in a way that allowed the occupant to be uncomfortable in a variety of miserable positions. Since I was only a mile away, I went to the hospital often to visit and bring Holy Communion. I was deeply touched by Jeremiah, the new communicant, and the hope and joy of the family. Jeremiah loved cars and was crazy about motorcycles. The walls were plastered with kids' art and school greeting cards, but wherever there was a blank space it was wallpapered with a picture of a hot rod or a Harley.

Through the weeks and months at the hospital that seemed endless, I began to notice that whenever I saw Kateri, Jeremiah's little sister, she had a blank stare and lost puppy look.

She was scared and hurting and worried about her big brother. She was also out of the limelight as everyone brought gifts and cards for Jeremiah and inquired into his well-being. Mary and Gary and her teachers tried to keep a sense of routine for her, but that was not really possible. Kateri was a "lost child" in the midst of the hospital mayhem. One day I thought, "I need to make her feel important." I decided to get a box of candy at Merb's, a St. Louis sweets shop, and have the delicacies wrapped beautifully. I brought it to the hospital and thought that I could flatter Kateri with the gift and make her feel generous and important at the same time.

"Kateri," I said, "Look, I brought you a gift." The lights in her eyes went on as she reached out to take it. She was in kindergarten and had probably never seen candy this precious that some pieces were wrapped in gold foil. She ripped off the paper and opened the box. Her jaw dropped open in disbelief as she viewed the artistry of the candy laid out like a jeweler's display case. She showed it to her mom and offered her a piece as she took one herself. After a few pieces were shared, I made a somewhat risky suggestion knowing that this would test her unselfishness. "Kateri, what would you think about taking the box of candy to the nurses' station and telling them to have some. You could tell them that this is your way of saying thank you for the good care that they give your brother." She did it without hesitation and the nurses were so thoughtful that they took a few pieces and told her to bring the box back to the room for later to have some to share when her grandparents came. It went as I had hoped. Kateri knew her specialness. She had not been ignored in the great concern for her brother. Kateri was the catalyst for this extended family's feeling of joy and gratitude even in this pressure cooker setting of the hospital.

As Jeremiah's stay dragged on, Mary wanted to have a healing prayer service with a drum circle. Once more, I was in that lovely chapel which had become so much a part of my visitation routine when I came to the hospital. I came so often that on a couple of occasions I was asked to be the celebrant for the daily Mass in Cardinal Glennon's chapel. People from the family, doctors and staff from the hospital, and parishioners from St. Cronan's came to be part of the drum circle ceremony. Several tom toms and larger drums were set up in the center aisle. Regrettably, Jeremiah could not attend the drumming in the chapel as he could not be released from the Intensive Care Unit. The pulsating life rhythm of the drumbeat echoed in the marble House of God with its terrazzo floors and stained glass windows. Rainbow sunbeams glared off the glossy floor in the late afternoon. We were pleading with the God who breathed life into the clay figure in Eden to breathe healing into Jeremiah, replacing the cancer cells with healthy ones. It remains a mystery how God moved that day and how the ceremony moved some participants to tears. It was reassuring to have distinguished medical staff and administrators pray with the family. On that first visit, I was concerned and intimidated with the very idea of being the priest visiting a child. By now, I had been elevated to the status of family priest. As the drumming concluded and I watched the circle of people depart, it occurred to me that Kateri was named for St. Kateri Tekawitha, the Lily of the Mohawks, the first Native American saint. In a totally different setting I was often the priest who prayed with Gary's co-workers who were the officers of the Salvation Army.

Once at my behest, Archbishop Raymond Burke came to the hospital to visit with Jeremiah. Since his mother wasn't there at the time, Archbishop Burke called her on the phone from Jeremiah's bedside. It was a lovely gesture. It wasn't my custom to request my archbishop visit all of the sick I visited in hospitals, but this one time I made an exception. Archbishop Burke had just been assigned to St. Louis. He was visiting the priests in various areas of the city, and when he came to a meeting in our community, we talked over a glass of wine and some crackers and cheese, the appropriate dish for a new bishop from Wisconsin. He mentioned, "I know I've met you before, but I've forgotten what parish you're in." Since ours is a small and humble parish immediately south of the magnificent and ornate St. Louis Cathedral Basilica, I thought that I would get his attention with some hyperbole. "I'm at St. Cronan's to the south of the Cathedral and the most important ministry in the whole St. Louis diocese is located in our parish boundaries." At that his jaw went slack and his eyes expressed disbelief and wonder. He was a short, sturdy and stocky Wisconsin farmer who froze at my pronouncement. I continued, "Yes, the most important work of the church in St. Louis is Cardinal Glennon Memorial Hospital for Children, the first Catholic children's hospital in the United States. Sometime soon I'm sure you'll go to visit there. But if you go right now, you could visit one of my parishioners, Jeremiah Busiek, who has a brain tumor. That way, when you pray with a child there, no one will think that you are merely going there to inspect the real estate." He listened and then turned his attention to some other priest whom he may have felt was going to be less demanding, but whatever the situation, he did visit. He did it so cavalierly that no hospital authority knew he was coming and his first visit to Cardinal Glennon Hospital as Archbishop didn't even become a photographic opportunity.

I was dumbfounded when I arrived in Jeremiah's room later that day. Gary said, "Did you bump into Archbishop Burke on the elevator? He just left here."

"No, I didn't. He must have been on the down elevator while I was on the up one." I was thrilled and pleased that I had taken the time to write out the name and room number for him after I had made the suggestion that he visit. I sent him a note when Jeremiah died, but I'm sure he had a more crowded calendar so he wasn't able to come to the funeral.

Early on, I told the Busiek family the story of Chris Page and our encounter with Dr. Ben Carson. Of course he had made very positive comments about Cardinal Glennon, and I told the story to bolster everyone's confidence. However, it was becoming clear that Jeremiah was slipping away and there was no prospect for recovery short of a miracle. Valentine's Day was a Saturday and Jeremiah had a four-legged Valentine that he loved very much. The anxiety and the stress were becoming more palpable; everyone longed for some relief. Jeremiah's aunt suggested that we get permission to bring Bandit, the family dog, to the hospital for a visit. She took Bandit to the groomer for a shampoo and trim before bringing him to the hospital that afternoon. Jeremiah sat in his wheelchair and Bandit was on his best behavior for petting and putting his chin and nose on Jeremiah's lap.

Bandit wasn't very noisy, but he did show some restrained excitement. Bandit spoke a few subdued woofs. Bandit didn't get Merb's Candy, but did get some Milk Bones for his excellent behavior. After all, he didn't get a shampoo and blow dry on any ordinary Saturday, he was a working dog chasing squirrels in the backyard. He also worked at playing with the kids. Jeremiah needed the visit and Bandit was a hit with the staff on the floor. He had to be kept isolated from the other children with their weakened immune systems. Bandit is not a trained therapy dog with a role in the hospital, but he was the right Valentine therapy for Jeremiah. Bandit was not Lassie or Rin Tin Tin star material, but no boy and his dog ever had a more poignant love affair. Bandit was at his very best, but it was clear that Jeremiah's best days were in the past. Even with this surprise visitor, Jeremiah was fragile and delicate. The cancer and the medicine kept him in a dazed state.

On March 7, 2004, a Sunday, Jeremiah died. I had finished Mass at the parish and stopped at the house before going to the parish hall for donuts and coffee. There was this message on the answering machine. "Jeremiah has died, please come to the hospital as soon as you get this message." It was a choking message interrupted with sobs, voice cracks and tense pauses. Gary had lost a beloved son just as God had and once more there were tears in heaven. As I backed my car out of the garage my heart was heavy and relieved. Thoughts of that strained first day of hesitant visiting percolated through my mind.

I found a parking spot near the door, rushed to the elevator and stopped to talk with the nurses at the nurses' station. I wanted a bit of background on his last hours. I also needed a bit of breathing space between Sunday Mass where we had just prayed for the family and this challenging moment of letting go. One of the nurses told me, "You don't have time to visit here. Gary and Mary are hoping that you would come soon because they want you to help them to bath Jeremiah's body." I was so touched and felt the tears in my eyes threatening to float out my contacts lenses. It was such a sacred moment. I had not baptized, Jeremiah, but I had anointed him several times. I would now baptize him into eternal life in the company of his parents who had loved him into life in this world. I entered the room and embraced them. We cried holding each other in a group hug beside the bed where Jeremiah's lifeless body lay. The constant struggle had ended and he was so at peace. Throughout my recent month of visiting him in his agony, he had been resilient and courageous. He was never a quitter. Now the constant effort for another lucid moment was over. He was in the hands of God who had raised up Jesus after His courageous struggle. Now fuzzy lucidity was replaced by brilliant luminescence in the unimagined radiance of God's face. One of the prefaces at the Mass for the Dead says, "We will see God and we will become like God." Jeremiah's face reflected the divine.

We proceeded with the task at hand with Mary washing the dear body of Jeremiah, flesh from her flesh, as Gary supported and held Jeremiah in position. I followed with the towel patting him as gently as I patted the dripping heads and faces of freshly baptized infants. It was reverent; it was slow, still, silent; all of us doing what we had never done before with profound homage for the sacred and tender teamwork. After dressing him in underwear we wrapped him in a soft blue blanket and placed him in Mary's arms in a rocking chair. The view from the third floor was of a blustery March day in St. Louis. The leafless trees had not yet awoken to new life, and the chill wind whistled. The sky was azure and rays of sunshine poured through the glass. Mary sat in a rocker bathed in an aura of sun shining from above as it had shined on Mary the Mother of Jesus. She silently welcomed people in the family who came in hushed procession to see the mother and child. No one could watch without thinking both of a Christmas card Madonna and Child and the harsh sword-piercing of the Pieta.

I hovered off to the side like an invisible guardian angel as family and loved ones, who had come in large numbers during the prolonged illness, now came once more to love and touch, hug and kiss in wordless solemnity.

I stepped outside and found Jeremiah's physician, Dr. O'Connor, in the hall. He had been such a stalwart caregiver and prayer partner throughout the entire ordeal, even coming to the drum ceremony. "Doctor, I'm sure you've seen this more than most people. I hear that parents who lose a child frequently see their marriage break up soon after."

"Father, that's right," he said, "but my experience is that good marriages get better and endure through the heartbreak. Marriages that are on the rocks already, collapse in the face of this pain. Parents have so much guilt over the loss of a child and sometimes they blame the other. The situation is so strained and pressure-packed. My guess is that this family will do fine. I'm very impressed with them. Of course, that's just my best guess and nobody but God knows." It would be hard to imagine anything that is more intense and heart-wrenching than having to bury your own child. I hoped that it would bring them even closer.

I couldn't leave the hospital without stopping by the chapel once more. Jesus was still there by the riverside blessing and watching over the kids. This visit was not as perplexing as my visit on that first day. Jesus was watching over Jeremiah, our special child in glory. Jesus had walked with me during all those months and both were watching over me now. At moments like this, the veil between this life and the next is thin and transparent. The mural was alive and the children of all hues were dancing around Jesus. I imagined that the heavenly scene had Mother Mary caressing Jeremiah just as Mary his mother held him close in death.

Jeremiah's parents asked me to celebrate the funeral Mass. The pastor and staff at St. Joseph's Parish were very accommodating. The school principal had visited often, and she was eager to help with the funeral plans and involve the whole school.

I drove the twenty miles to the parish appreciating the solitude of the ride and wondering if I ever could have envisioned the situation. It was March 11th and I was going to have an innocent child's funeral on the thirty-seventh anniversary of my ordination to the priesthood. It is best that life is full of surprises, because it would be unbearable if we knew ahead of time what was around the next corner. The selection of the scriptures for the Mass was made easy and obvious in one aspect. We would read the Book of the Prophet Jeremiah, his patron and namesake.

> Now the word of the Lord came to me saying, "Before I formed you in the womb I knew you, and before you were born I consecrated you; I appointed you a prophet to the nations."
> Then I said, "Ah, Lord God! Truly I do not know how to speak, for I am only a boy." But the Lord said to me, "Do not say, 'I am only a boy'; for you shall go to all to whom I send you, and you shall speak whatever I command you,
> Do not be afraid of them for I am with you to deliver you, says the Lord."
> JER. 1:4-8

Jeremiah was a strong little boy who was gallant and steadfast like the ancient prophet who preceded him. I don't know what I said in the funeral homily, but the comments later convinced me that the Spirit works in feeble instruments. The listeners had ears to hear whatever God moved me to say. A final word was added by the principal, Miss Patricia Kirk, who read this poem that was discovered in Jeremiah's locker. On a preprinted page entitled "I AM LOVABLE"... Jeremiah wrote, "I am nice...I am funny...I am good...I am holy...I am cold."

I drove back to the parish after this exhausting thirty-seventh ordination anniversary and spent the rest of the afternoon in church trying to process the drama of the months spent with Jeremiah and his family. It resembled the introduction I had to Lauren Blumenthal's family except for the obvious difference and the most important fact: Lauren lived. There was a second, less telling factor to the larger community, which included the daily headlines regarding priestly child abuse and the role that played in the St. Cronan situation. In my replay and evaluation of the entire Jeremiah situation, it was obvious that the pressure of being a priest in regular contact with an especially vulnerable child was tedious and depressing. As the situation played itself out over the months of Jeremiah's sickness and his family's loving embrace of me, it was inconsequential. Once I got over that initial hurdle on the first day in the hospital visiting area, I was home free; but I was tense and intimidated from the beginning.

Months went by and I became aware that there was still one more chapter to the story. Jeremiah's parents felt a deep bond for Cardinal Glennon Hospital and especially for the staff in the oncology unit. Periodically, the family would prepare an evening meal for the cancer unit. However, the bigger picture that was emerging involved a significant gift to the hospital. The Busiek's experience taught them that the crowded rooms were much too confining. And when a child is really sick, the Ronald McDonald House is too far away. In a critical situation, the house two blocks away seemed like two hundred miles. They decided to use money people had donated to a memorial fund in Jeremiah's honor to build a family room on the fourth floor oncology unit of the hospital where Jeremiah lived his last days. The Jeremiah Room would have a living room with a foldout sofa bed, a kitchen table, a desk with a computer, bookshelf with toys and games for siblings, and a real Lazy Boy recliner. There would be no impostor Lazy Boy that imposed cruel and unusual punishment rather than rest. Every inch of the build out and the selection of the furniture required study and approval by a multi-layered hospital bureaucracy. Progress was so slow and so many approvals required that Mary and Gary were beginning to wonder if their idea was attractive to the hospital or their own pipe dream. Just when they were thinking that the comparison with turtles and snails and glaciers was an insult to the speed of these, approval came and the new area was developed. The new furnishings had to be so clean as to be kept germ free.

The room was in the area where Bandit had visited on Valentine's Day. Gary and Mary called me to schedule a Sunday to bless the room. In this large institutional setting, the Jeremiah Room was a cozy island retreat. Kateri was proud that she was able to select the toys and children's books to round out the décor and make it family-friendly. Once more we used the reading from the Prophet Jeremiah for the ceremony and I inscribed the bible I donated to the bookshelf for the use of families who would come to the room for some breathing space and solace. Burying your child is intense and draining, caring for others with a sick child fills a person with healing even amidst the lingering heartache.

Jeremiah Truetken-Busiek

Vitals: Born 9/11/94; Baptized 1/15/95; First Communion 6/18/02 at Cardinal Glennon Memorial Hospital; Died March 7, 2004. He made his First Communion before his operation on the day I first visited with his family. He refrained from further Holy Communion in that early hospitalization period because he wanted to wait for his formal "First Communion" with his grade school class. Jeremiah's story could have made a lesser family bitter; Jeremiah's life made all of us who knew him – better.

CONCLUSION

MICHAEL POTTER

THE LAST WORD

"In the beginning was the Word
and the Word was with God and the Word was God."

JOHN 1:1

IN THE FINAL MONTHS OF WRITING THIS BOOK, I was reworking the chapter on Natalie West. While I paused to reread a sentence and search for a better word, the name, Michael Potter, flashed into my consciousness. I was startled by this lightening bolt of instant recall of a name that I had not thought about in over twenty years and of a boy I barely remembered. If I had ever believed in the Spirit's enlightenment or karma, I did at that very moment of deliberation: Michael Potter... Michael Potter... Michael Potter? I scratched my head and pondered about this boy, Michael Potter. Who is Michael Potter? I knew that stumbling on this name, Michael Potter, at this very moment was a pearl of great price even though the boy himself was vague and shadowy in my mind. I racked my brain and recalled a bare inkling here and a hint there, but as vague and fuzzy as it all was, I was sure I was on to something important. I was carefully unpacking a box that hopefully contained a beautiful family portrait but it was still hidden in the bubble wrap. I had a deep nagging notion about the importance of this boy to my current writing endeavor, but there was no clarity of detail. I was in a fog regarding Michael Potter, but I knew that when the light broke through it would be a beautiful new day. I only hoped that when the total story emerged at that illustrious moment of achievement and insight I would be supremely confident about concluding my book, "THE END."

I sat back and closed my eyes and let the name float through my peaceful mind and slowly an image of Michael Potter started to emerge like a picture torn from the back of a Polaroid Land Camera. I was dizzy with joy and anticipation and rattled with self-doubt. I was the miner with the gold nugget cocky about uncovering the mother lode. This Michael Potter was a find of prime importance but strangely I felt that I had only known him for fifteen seconds. A few of the memories slowly organized themselves in my consciousness like a critical mass. Then a whole flood of recollections followed with the color and texture of Michael and his story. I had a gnawing suspicion that my previous book, *THE PEOPLE PARISH*, was the super glue uniting these many fragments. I knew in my gut that Michael had read my book.

I challenged myself with the tantalizing question, How in the world was I ever going to verify who Michael Potter was and the truth of the Michael Potter story that was now tantalizingly close? The Michael Potter in my recollections was dead, and I couldn't change that tragic truth. I could go paging through the volumes of my old journals, but I didn't have a hint as to where I would begin. In fact, my journals were not kept in any orderly sequence as the Encyclopedia Britannica was on my bookshelf. I knew that Michael Potter was a part of my life during the St. Bridget's years, but that only narrowed it down to the ten years from 1985 – 95. Then another dazzling aha moment came in a name: Father Finbarr!

If all of my ruminations about Michael Potter were not fantasy, the person who would know the whole story was Benedictine Father Finbarr Dowling, who was at the St. Louis Priory School for many years. He taught a senior social justice class and used my book, *THE PEOPLE PARISH*, as required reading in the course. Yes, I will call Father Finbarr, who is now the pastor of St. Ignatius Parish in remote Concord Hill, MO. I dialed the phone and waited anxiously hoping to get more than an answering machine. The English Benedictine answered with a crisp soft, gentle but authoritative voice that still retained a slight accent.

I began, "Hello, Father Finbarr, this is Gerry Kleba at St. Cronan's Parish." We did exchange a few pleasantries but I was eager to continue.

"I haven't talked to you in years, and I'm really not going to give you any hint as to the reason why I am calling now." I consciously forced a smile on my face because I heard that caused a more pleasant aura and tone and would likely evoke a positive response. I needed the right energy field to surround my words knowing that energy attracts energy. "I have a question for you. This may seem to come out of left field, but please tell me what you know. Who was Michael Potter, and why does Michael Potter have any connection with me?" I asked the question slowly to give this studious Benedictine the time to shift back a few decades to my era of concern.

As I awaited an answer I was holding my breath. It would have been terribly embarrassing if he had said, "Gerry, I don't have the slightest idea about the two of you or what you might be talking about or the truth is I don't think I even know anyone named Michael Potter."

To my delight Finbarr dove into answering my question without the slightest pause; it was effortless instant recall. It was as though he had just spoken about Michael over morning tea. He was speedier than a Jeopardy contestant who had dominated the show for a week. "Gerry," I loved his creamy British accent, "Michael Potter was a student at the St. Louis Priory School in 1989. In the spring of that year, he went on a trip with some of his classmates to Mexico. After his return home on the airplane, he decided to drive over and visit with his girlfriend that he had not seen in a week. He left her house late that night and when he was a mile from home he fell asleep at the wheel, crashed the car and died in a fiery accident." So far the report was as I had remembered it, but with more details than I ever knew.

He continued, "The funeral was a shocking school event, and it was impossibly traumatic for his entire family and his mother, Patsy, who was overcome with grief." Finbarr continued, "Sometime after the funeral, Patsy, came to school to clean out his locker and gather up his personal belongings. It was during that time she discovered the paper that Michael had written as a report for my class. In the paper, Michael wrote about his admiration for you. He desired to be like you even though he didn't feel any call to be a priest. So that's the Michael Potter story and the way the two of you are connected."

When Finbarr reassured me that all of my memory fragments were accurate I filled him in on my reason for the call. I told him how this phone conversation had made my day and about the book I was currently writing, and how important it was to use this story as the closing chapter of the book. I said, "I seem to remember that Michael had a younger brother who went up on stage to receive Michael's diploma."

Finbarr spouted out the brothers' names as if he had a class seating chart in his hand as we talked. "He has an older brother, Brian, who was a graduate of the Priory and a younger brother, Tim, who was the boy who received Michael's diploma."

I told him how I remembered the visit with Patsy some time later on. "She came down to St. Bridget's accompanied by another Benedictine priest, Father Andrew Wimmer. Andrew had a brother, Peter, who was a senior at the Priory, a close friend of Michael's and one of the boys on the Mexican holiday. Patsy was still numb from the tragedy, but needed to visit the priest in Michael's essay. Given her heartbroken state and the shattered state of the St. Bridget neighborhood, she wasn't about to make a trip to the housing projects alone. She brought down a half dozen of Michael's senior pictures and on each of them he was poised, elegant, and exuded a joyful radiance. These could have been the cover photos on GQ for the next six months running. I remember that Patsy told me stories about his life and aspirations and his delight in meeting me.

I told her that I had really only met her son in person during the day that Finbarr brought the class down to my parish in the downtown housing projects for a field trip and to encounter poverty and black people first hand. He drove the students downtown avoiding the interstate, which was the path that their parents always took in driving them to see the Cardinals at Busch Stadium. Part of the experience included coming downtown on all the ghetto streets lined with boarded up buildings, burned out shells and vacant lots peopled with men huddled around fires in 55-gallon drums outside liquor stores holding their bottles in brown paper bags.

These streets were littered with broken bottles and food wrappers in the gutter and lined with shabby houses with unscreened windows with tattered curtains billowing out the openings like sails in the America's Cup Race. Sometimes there were youngsters dangling out in precarious positions on window sills less secure than the blowing curtains on their rods.

During the field trip, I took them to a homeless shelter with a meal program, to a job training program, to our school to meet Sister Gail, the principal, and finally to the urban garden next to the school where our students learned some horticulture. It was equally important they learned that the earth grows food in dirt rather than believing it comes from a market in plastic shrink wrap. We concluded this crammed day by celebrating a Mass after which they went home. When they left church, I stood at the front doorway, shook each student's hand and thanked them. Some had a last minute question and the other frustrated students hoped I would give a brief answer because they were eager to return to their forested campus and suburban homes. That was when my forgotten moment of personal encounter with Michael Potter occurred. At the time, I never knew him much less suspected his admiration for me.

"Finbarr, maybe I never told you this, but at that meeting with Patsy, she told me that she wanted to give me a gift. She said, 'Father, we have all this money that we were going to spend on Michael's college education. But now we won't need it for that. Since Michael admired you so much, I want to give you some of the money to use to educate children at your school.' Then she surprised me giving me a generous check, which was a big help in our inner-city grade school. Before she left, we prayed together, and then I showed them to the door. I was tempted to take them to church or over to school to meet Sister Gail, but for some reason I didn't do that. I would always have done that but in this instance I thought that the trip to my house was itself enough of an excursion into a different world for one day. Maybe there would be another time.

Finbarr and I concluded our conversation and I was euphoric. I hung up the phone but my silent satisfaction was tainted with bittersweet memories. The Spirit had shockingly blessed me by dropping the name and story of Michael Potter on me like Juan Diego had gotten the roses in December and the picture on his tilma while he was out for a walk. I wasn't expecting to encounter Michael Potter anymore than he was expecting to meet Our Lady of Guadalupe. Now Finbarr assured me that the details of the encounter were not idle machinations of a wandering mind but a true, icing on the cake story to conclude my book.

With the help of the development office at the Priory, I traced down Michael's mother, Patsy, and she was delighted to know that Michael was being remembered in this way. Patsy searched through her treasures and found the final paper that Michael wrote. This is what he said. "I liked Father Kleba's book, *THE PEOPLE PARISH*, because it was alive with stories about real people in situations that were foreign to me even though they were St. Louis stories. I liked him when I met him and heard about his vision to build a scholar house for neighborhood kids to live together while going to college and tutor youngsters in the neighborhood. I don't think I have a priestly vocation, but I want to be like Father Kleba and help the poor in some way."

THE END

EPILOGUE

POSSIBLY THIS BOOK LEAVES YOU PLEADING, even demanding, "Tell me another story." If so, I believe these stories have sparked your memory and warmed your heart in a way that has made you recall a similar situation, either when you mentored a child or when you were a valued child warmly embraced. I urge you to write your own story of a sacred relationship with a child or about the adult who inspired and helped form you as a child and make you more of a child of God. Send it to the person you cherish. Fight off the anxiety and fear of rejection and invite a response. Be energized with the awakening of a lost friendship or the deepening of a friendship that has persisted, but longs to be rekindled. This God's Children Project will be a seed to enhance widespread intergenerational bonding and heal brokenness, one relationship at a time. Rather than me telling you another story, I would love to have your story in my collection. Send it to: gerry@stcronan.org.